Hearing is Not Enough:

A Guide to Being a Better Listener

ISBN-13: 978-1-7324823-9-5

Hearing is Not Enough:

A Guide to Being a Better Listener

Brandy Champeau and Nancy Holt

Exploring Expression LLC

Also by Brandy Champeau

90 Days to Your Better Expression: A Journal Experience

100 Things I Didn't Know Before: My Learning Journal

Children's Books by Brandy Champeau

Tip and Ben Find a Friend

Dandelion's Magic

The Last Elephant Parade

Terrence the Saddest Stallion

Little Lion Makes a Roar

Table of Contents

Introduction   1

1   What is Communication?   7

2   Listening: A Necessary Skill   25

3   What is (and is not) Listening   35

4   Determining Your Listening Style   45

5   WHY are you Listening?   57

6   5 Types of Listening   67

7   Barriers to Effective Listening   85

8   Feedback   101

9   Listening with Your Eyes   117

10   HOW to Improve Your Listening Skills   139

11   A Few Last Words About Effective Listening   151

Appendix   157

Glossary   173

Index   183

Introduction

"WHILE THE RIGHT TO TALK MAY BE THE BEGINNING OF FREEDOM, THE NECESSITY OF LISTENING IS WHAT MAKES THE RIGHT IMPORTANT." - Walter Lippmann

When was the last time you really felt listened to? Even more important, when was the last time you really listened to someone else? Think about the relationships in your life. How many times have conflicts and arguments arisen because of a simple breakdown in communication? This communication bond is so difficult to forge and so easily broken. Yet, communication is little more than someone speaking and someone listening. The issue becomes, in this fast-paced world of ours, that we spend far more time speaking than we do listening. Therefore, our speaking muscles grow strong, while our listening muscles wither. We need to change this.

Technology has brought an astounding amount of information to everyone. In the past, Grandma and Grandpa would have to go to a local library, search through card catalogs to find sources, and then hunt down the volumes of reference books. A person's access to information was frequently limited by the size of their town's budget for the library. Today we simply turn on our phones or laptops and find what we want to know in seconds while sitting in our living rooms or cars or anywhere.

The accessibility to immediate abundant information produces more knowledge and more opinions than ever before. And, at least in our society, people have the right to speak and be heard. In fact, in America, we value the freedom to speak so much that it is included the first amendment to our constitution. But here's the question: shouldn't the right to speak and be heard include the reciprocal? With rights come an inherent responsibility to honor and respect those same rights in others. Thus, the right to be heard carries a responsibility to listen. If we expect people to listen to us when we speak, we, as a people, need to be more prepared–more equipped — to listen to others when they speak.

This book was conceived to explore the responsibility we take on with our right to speak. Listening is the debt we owe each other. The fabric of society and the relationships we have with each other depend on our ability to listen with the appropriate level of care and skill. You can't build a positive and lasting relationship with someone without some form of respect in place. Tantamount to that respect is the idea that you will listen to me and I will listen to you. Unfortunately, we all too often work on the you should listen to me part. The "I listen to you" gets neglected and becomes rusty.

Listening is both an art and a skill. Why and how we choose to employ listening is as important to the passing of a message as the reason and methods behind speaking. When was the last time you considered **WHY** you listen to someone?   How often do you think about **HOW** you are listening to someone?   Perhaps some of the miscommunication we all experience in our lives are less a matter of a transmission and more a matter of reception.

This book is about more than the simple idea of proper listening. If I've learned anything in all of my years of communication and education, it is this: communication is about relationships. Without the relationship between two people there would be no need for listening.   It is the presence of or the desire for a relationship that makes us want to listen to each other.   And, even more important, if we don't listen to each other, relationships will fail.   This is true for people, for families and for nations.

Without the relationship between two people there would be no need for listening.

Hearing is not enough. For relationships to grow and prosper, we must truly listen to each other. This is why this book exists. Our desire for you as you read this book, is that you begin to examine the role listening plays in your life. At the end of most of the chapters we will be looking at listening within the context of the different types of relationships that we have in our lives. We will examine how listening, whether active or passive, can affect the development of our many relationships. When we utilize intentional, active listening we help those relationships grow in a positive manner. We will also be giving you specific and actionable steps that you can take to build and strengthen your listening muscles.

Hearing is not enough. For relationships to grow and prosper, we must truly listen to each other.

The question to ask yourself as you take this journey with us is not "Am I being listened to?". We don't even want you to ask, "Have I been listening?" Most people listen to someone sometimes. No, here are the questions we want you to ask yourself as you read this book:

- Am I listening as often as I should?
- Am I listening as effectively as I could?
- How can I improve my listening so that I can improve my relationships?

We hope *Hearing is Not Enough* will be your guide as you take steps to grow as a listener. This will be a journey. The path to effective listening will take you through understanding your own listening style, figuring out WHY you listen, learning the proper type of listening to use for different situations and applying appropriate feedback. By the end of this book you will be well on your way to being the kind of listener that people **want** to talk to.

There is an old quote by Epictitus that goes, "We have two ears and one mouth so we can listen twice as much as we speak." And yet so much of our education and training is focused on speaking. Let this book help you change that. With this book, it is our hope, that you will become even better at using your two ears for real, active listening–not just hearing.

"WE HAVE TWO EARS AND ONE MOUTH SO WE CAN LISTEN TWICE AS MUCH AS WE SPEAK" - Epicitus

The Path to Better Listening

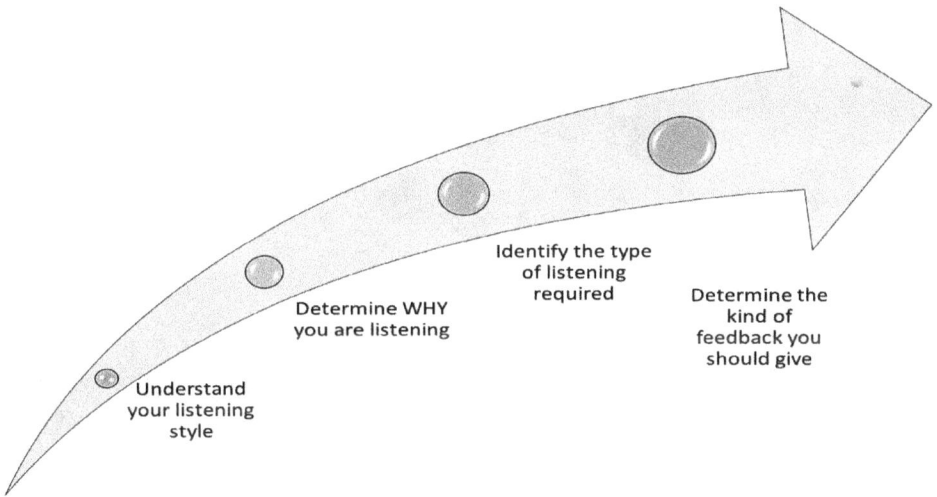

Identify the type
of listening
required

Determine WHY
you are listening

Determine the
kind of
feedback you
should give

Understand
your listening
style

Chapter 1:

What is Communication?

"GOOD COMMUNICATION IS THE BRIDGE BETWEEN CONFUSION AND CLARITY" - Nat Turner

When my children were babies, I would often hear them cry from their cribs. The moment the sound of their wails reached my ears I would attach meaning to it. I learned to differentiate between the cry of hunger, the cry of tired and the cry of hurt. Even before my children learned to talk to me, I was learning to listen to them. We were communicating.

Communication is what separates us from rocks. The ability to communicate with each other, that is the ability to engage in the deliberate transfer of a meaningful message, helps to form the fabric of civilization.

One person does or says something, thereby engaging in symbolic behavior. Others observe what was done or said and attribute meaning to it. Whenever you observe or give meaning to behavior, communication is taking place. Something is occurring, spurred by one person, and a message is sent. Another person receives the message and communication has occurred.

> ***Whenever you observe or give meaning to behavior, communication is taking place.***

As humans, though, we have the ability to take things one step further. We are able to communicate through language. We use language to communicate our meanings and pass our messages.

Communication can take on two forms:

- Intrapersonal communication - communication with yourself
- Interpersonal communication – communication with others

Intrapersonal Communication

Intrapersonal communication is the communication we have with ourselves. It is our inner monologue.

Have you ever seen those images of the person with an angel on one shoulder and a devil on the other? Both small beings are trying to convince the person to make a decision in their favor. This is an example of intrapersonal communication. Both the little angel and the little devil are aspects of the same person. He is not having a conversation with another person. He is actually dialoging with himself.

Intrapersonal communication requires only a single communicator −**You!** People often employ intrapersonal communication to calm themselves down in a stressful situation or to hype themselves up before an important event. If you have ever laughed at a personal joke you were engaged in a form of intrapersonal communication.

Interpersonal Communication

Interpersonal communication is the communication that we have with someone else. It requires two people.

Interpersonal communication happens when one person (a sender) transmits a message to another person (a receiver) *and the other person receives it.*

Without that second person, the receiver, you don't have an interpersonal communication exchange. In fact, you don't really have communication at all.

I remember a few years back I had to give a couple of workshops at a conference. My first workshop was packed with people. Messages were sent. Messages were received. Communication flowed like a river. My second workshop though was different. There was nobody there. It was empty enough I could have heard crickets chirping — if there had been crickets. Which there wasn't; not even the crickets came to this workshop. It was just me, speaking to an empty room. I spoke for an hour with no real communication taking place. Why? Because there was no receiver to catch my message. There can't be interpersonal communication without someone to listen.

To function, true interpersonal communication requires the **relationship** between the people in whatever form it may exist. We will get into more about relationships in just a bit. However, the idea that we really want you to get here is that if you are looking for more than an inner monologue, then it takes two to communicate.

Without that second person, the receiver, you don't have an interpersonal communication exchange.

Communication as a Relational Bond

Think for a moment about your life. Who are you in a relationship with? If you are like most people, your mind immediately went to your spouse or significant other. If you are single, perhaps your initial response was "no one", or "myself". However, the romantic relationship you share with your spouse is only one of the many relationships you possess right now.

Throughout your life you form hundreds and thousands of interpersonal relationships. An interpersonal relationship refers to the association, connection, interaction, and bond between two or more people. These relationships are established and defined as we communicate with each other.

Interpersonal relationships can take the form of:

- Acquaintances/Strangers
- Professional relationships
- Friendships
- Family relationships
- Romantic relationships

Acquaintances

Aquaintances are people you know slightly but who are not close friends.   These could be presenters or classmates in a lecture hall or friends of your friends.   Acquaintances also include strangers you encounter and speak with.   These may be people such as the cashier at the store, the people at the next table in a restaurant, or a person you meet while walking through a park.

Professional Relationships

Professional or work relationships are formed with people with whom you have a professional connection. This could include not only your coworkers but also your supervisors or subordinates. Clients, customers, and vendor representatives also would fall into this category.

Friendships

Friends are people whom we are not related to but choose to interact with on a regular basis. Friends are people we trust, respect, care about and feel we can confide in and want to spend time with. A good friendship should be built on honesty, support, and loyalty. A friendship is a reciprocal relationship, however. For it to exist, both people must see each other as a friend. Friends typically are mutually respectful and supportive and share common interests and ideas.

Family Relationships

Family relationships refer to the people to whom you are connected to through some form of kinship, whether it is through blood, marriage, romantic relationships, or adoption. This could include the parent-child relationship, the brother-sister relationship, the in-law relationship or many others.

Family relationships are usually life-long, although they can and frequently do evolve over time. An example of this is when children become teenagers and then adults. As this occurs the parent-child relationship evolves to become less one of guidance and more one of mutual support.

Strong and healthy communication with family members is crucial as, if a healthy relationship is nurtured, a family can be a lifelong source of support. The bond with a family plays an especially important role in personal and emotional wellbeing and the ability to form other kinds of relationships outside of the family unit such as friendships and romantic relationships.

Romantic Relationships

A **romantic relationship** is one in which you feel very strongly attracted to the other person, both to their personality and, often, physically. This is reciprocated by the other person in the relationship. A romantic relationship is that which exists between a boyfriend and girlfriend (in a heterosexual relationship) or a boyfriend and boyfriend or girlfriend and girlfriend (in a homosexual relationship) or spouses (in a marriage) or life partners (in a civil partnership or long-term unmarried relationship).

A romantic relationship is the closest form of relationship and the two people involved will often describe themselves as being attracted to each other and/or "in love". Romantic relationships are defined in terms of the concepts of passion, intimacy, and commitment. The partners feel an incredibly strong connection and bond to each other that they do not feel with others, even close friends.

The Relationship Continuum

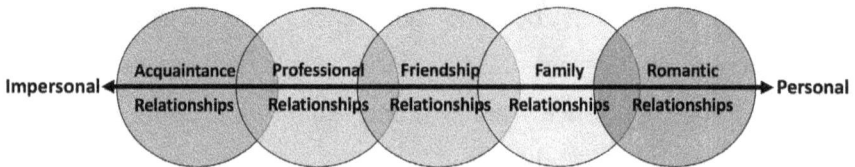

Impersonal ← Acquaintance Relationships | Professional Relationships | Friendship Relationships | Family Relationships | Romantic Relationships → Personal

The above interpersonal relationships exist on a continuum from impersonal to personal. At one end you have strangers and acquaintances. These types of relationships tend to be impersonal and perhaps fleeting. On the far other end of the spectrum exist your family and romantic relationships.

As we grow and evolve the nature of our relationship with a person can move back and forth along the continuum. If the relationship is healthy and nurtured it is possible to grow from acquaintance to friend or more.

Inversely, an unhealthy or improperly nurtured relationship can sour, and romantic partners or friends could become veritable strangers. Often it is the ability to engage in effective communication that determines the direction and path a relationship takes.

Where the relationship falls on the spectrum often plays a major role in the type of listening that we engage in and the eventual success of the communication itself. We may not listen as deeply or closely to someone with whom we share only an acquaintance relationship as we do to a person we share a romantic relationship with. We often need to engage in one type of listening with coworkers and another with family members.

These many relationships and the manner in which you manage them form one of the pillars on which emotional intelligence rests. As we proceed through this book, we want to look at listening within the constructs of these relationships. We hope to demonstrate just how important the skill of listening can be in the practice of positive relationship building. And just like any skill, with a little practice and refinement the skill of listening can help you build a firm foundation for your relationship pillar.

The Communication Model

As we move through this book and look at the many ways in which we can become better listeners we will be returning again and again to the communication model. The communication model provides a visual representation of the communication process — how the message goes from the sender to the receiver. The above graphic provides a simple example of the interpersonal communication model.

The success of a communication process depends on several factors:

- **The Sender (Mrs. S.).** This is the person sending the message. She has something she wants to communicate.
- **The Receiver (Mr. R.).** This is the intended recipient of Mrs. S's message. Whether or not he receives the intended message will depend on how well he can listen despite the noise or barriers present.
- **The nature of the message itself.** This is the message as the sender intends it. Will this be the same message that the receiver perceives?
- **The channel or mode of delivery.** This could include verbal, non-verbal or even written. For the purposes of this book we will be focusing on verbal channels, with the exception of one later chapter about nonverbal communication.
- **The barriers or noise present.** These are all of the things that get in the way of the passing of a message between the sender and receiver. These could be physical, psychological, semantic or biases.
- **The feedback sent in response.** This is the return message sent by the receiver. Feedback is how the sender knows that the message that they intended to throw was actually caught.

Since this book is about *Listening* and not about Talking, we will be focusing on the *receiver* and those portions of the communication process in which the receiver has a direct effect. These include the **receiver, the barriers present, and the feedback**.

Speech and the Role of Listening in Communication and Relationship Building

Relationships thrive on successful communication and successful communication is a partnership. Under normal circumstances, the person speaking is sending the message expecting the receiver to not just hear, but also listen to the message. They are doing their job as the sender and they have the expectation that the receiver will also be doing what needs to be done. Whether that message is to inform, to persuade or to entertain, the sender is communicating with the expectation of sending meaning. Based on the message being sent and the interpersonal relationship between the two people, the receiver needs to know and employ the listening methods, skills and degree of concentration needed to ensure the success of the message.

A quarterback in a football game does not throw the ball just anywhere. He aims the ball at a receiver and expects that person to do his job. The sender of a message has the same expectations. All they can do is aim the message and throw to the best of their ability. The rest is up to the receiver. **The question is what will you, as the receiver, do with the message that is sent?** Bearing this in mind, the rest of this book is focused on making you a better receiver of the information being sent your way.

Meet the Players

As we proceed through this listening journey, we intend to utilize six specific situations to better illustrate and help you understand the role of listening in context. As we look at different aspects of the scenarios through the lenses of our listening discussion and chapters, we pose many questions for your consideration. Some of the questions we will answer and some we will not. The point of these scenarios is to get you, the reader, to think critically about the application of the particular aspect of listening in various situations. These scenarios may be similar to a situation you would encounter in your own life. Just like in life — sometimes we don't get all of the answers.

The Players sections of this book are your chance to consider, practice, and draw your own conclusions about the information presented in the chapter. There are no wrong answers here. Remember, this book is about you. This is *your journey* to being a better listener. We are here merely to guide you. We hope that throughout this book

and through the course of witnessing the various interactions of the Smith family, you learn a little about yourself, a little bit about the relationships you share with other people and a lot about the role that listening can play in preserving and nurturing those relationships.

With that said, let's first set the stages and meet the various members of the Smith family.

Jarrod and Edna Smith (the romantic relationship)

Edna and Jarrod Smith have been married for 20 years. Jarrod is a lawyer and Edna is a systems analyst. They have two children together, Reggie who is 18 and Jasmine who is 15. Edna and Jarrod have a generally happy marriage, however it is not without its minor irritations. One of these centers around the trash.

In this interaction, Edna is standing at the living room doorway trying to pass a message to her husband, Jarrod. The message she is trying to pass is "Take out the trash." Her hands are on her hips and her eyebrows are forming a "V". Jarrod Smith is sitting in his recliner watching his favorite football team trample their opponent. "Honey, did you forget to take out the trash?" Edna asks.

Jasmine Smith and her mother, Edna (the family relationship)

Jasmine Smith is 15. She attends the local high school where she is well liked and active in sports and other activities. Jasmine has a generally good relationship with her parents.

Jasmine has just been asked out on her very first date. Brimming with excitement she approaches her mother for permission and advice. Edna Smith has just gotten home from work. She is in the kitchen preparing dinner when Jasmine bursts into the room.

Reggie Smith at college (the acquaintance relationship #1)

Reggie Smith, Jarrod and Edna's 18-year-old son, is in his first semester of college. He is very bright and did well in high school. He is looking forward to this new chapter of his life, however this is his first time living on his own, in a college dorm.

Reggie walks into his first class to discover a lecture hall filled with 150 other students. While he has great respect for his professor, Dr. Carter, the structure of the class prohibits anything more than an acquaintance level relationship. Reggie takes a seat several rows back from the front and gets out his notebook as class begins.

The Smith's go out to dinner (the acquaintance relationship #2)

It is Jarrod Smith's birthday. The family has decided to treat him to dinner at his favorite restaurant. Reggie has even made the trip back from college to help celebrate his father's special day. When they arrive, the restaurant is packed with diners. However, after only a brief wait, they are shown to their table.

Shortly after Jessica, the waitress, arrives to read them the specials and take their order. Jessica is a single mother with one son, Archie. She has been working at this restaurant for a couple of months and generally enjoys her job.

Edna Smith at the office (the work relationship)

Edna Smith is a system analyst at a mid-size computer firm. She has been selected to lead a new project with 2 of her coworkers, Pam and Tom. This is a particularly important, complex project. It is crucial that everyone do their part so that the project succeeds.

Edna is meeting with Pam and Tom today to kickoff and discuss the specifics of new project. This is the first time she has found herself in a lead position and is excited for the opportunity. She knows that this project could lead to bigger and better things for not only her, but Pam and Tom as well.

Jarrod Smith and his golf buddy (the friendship relationship)

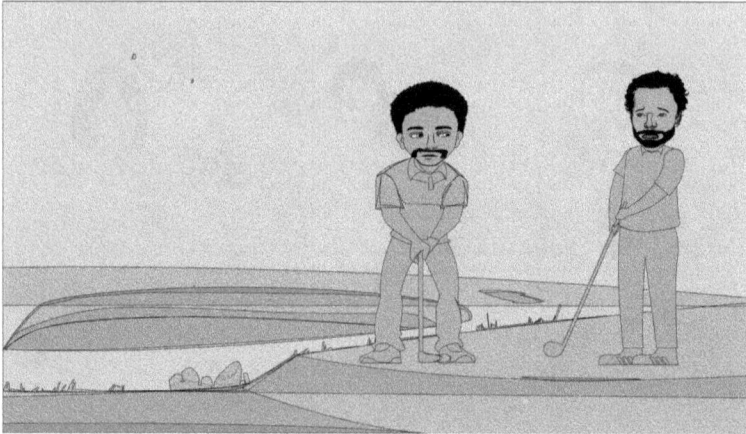

Jarrod is enjoying a round of golf with his friend, Mike. Jarrod and Edna have been friends with Mike and his wife, Lisa, for nearly a decade. Jarrod and Mike typically meet twice a month for golf and have been doing so for several years.

Lately, Mike has been going through a difficult period in his marriage. In fact, he and Lisa have been considering getting a divorce. Looking for support and advice, Mike has decided to bring up the situation with Jarrod during their golf game.

Chapter 2

Listening: A Necessary Skill

"TEACHING IS USELESS UNLESS YOU CAN LEARN
FROM YOUR STUDENTS" - Martin Dansky

I love conferences. If given the choice I would rather speak at a conference than almost anywhere else. This is not because I love speaking, although I do. This isn't because I love networking, although I enjoy that as well. No, I would rather speak at conferences because it allows me to sit in on other people's workshops and presentations. You see, conferences are about listening to and learning from each other. I firmly believe that if someone goes there just to speak and leave (which is sometimes unavoidable, I know) they are missing half of the beauty of the experience. They are missing out on the listening.

People spend between 70% and 80% of their day engaged in some form of communication, and about 55% of their time is devoted to listening.   This illustrates the idea that our bodies are hard-wired to listen more than we speak.

Talking Vs. Hearing

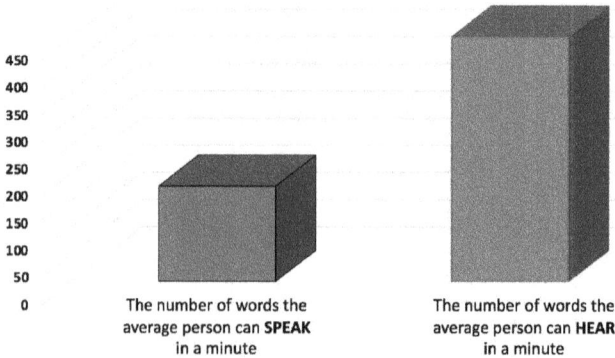

The number of words the average person can **SPEAK** in a minute

The number of words the average person can **HEAR** in a minute

Unfortunately, most of our attention is too often focused on what we are **talking about** as opposed to what we are **listening to**. Because of this too many of the messages sent our way only get heard and not actually listened to. Think about this — how many messages have you missed because you were not actually listening like you should?

What Happens to the Words we Hear?

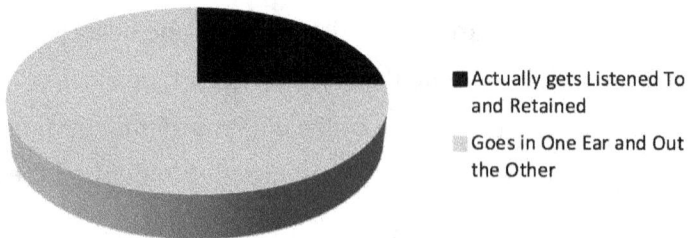

■ Actually gets Listened To and Retained

Goes in One Ear and Out the Other

Listening as a Necessity

As we reap the benefits of the information age and become more adept at receiving information digitally, we are reducing our opportunities to practice the important skill of listening. Yet... 80% of top executives believe listening is one of the most important skills needed in a corporate environment.

80% of top executives believe listening is one of the most important skills needed in a corporate environment.

Whether a good follower or a good leader, whether a medical student or law professional, whether an accountant or a programmer, or whether a spouse or a parent, good listening remains vital to your success. Listening shows the speaker that you respect them and value what they are saying. Good listening serves not only to improve our knowledge and understanding, but to help us build and maintain healthy relationships. In fact, it is impossible to have a successful conversation without a good listener. And there is a big difference between just a listener and a good listener.

It is impossible to have a successful conversation without a good listener.

Listening as a Skill

It is not difficult to listen, even children can do it. Some say that babies begin listening even before leaving the womb. This is why experts now suggest that you begin reading to your child in utero — before they are ever born. However, just because you've been listening since before you were born, doesn't mean you are good at it.

Listening is not just an ability; it is a skill. Think about it like singing. If you can open your mouth and raise and lower the pitch of your voice you are technically able to sing. But this doesn't mean that you can sing well. How do you take your voice from the sound of dying cats to true music that people want to hear? You work on it. Listening is just like this. Just because you can hear, does not make you a good listener.

As with any skill, **practice and attention** are required to become a skillful listener. Musicians, speakers, and writers often take formal training to develop their skills. Football and baseball players go through an intensive training prior to their games. People learning to play an instrument or play a sport are encouraged to practice, practice, and practice.

Unfortunately, however, *few of us have ever participated in formal listening training*. People who mention that they are working on learning to listen get quizzical looks from others. Most people assume that everyone knows how to listen. But, like we mentioned before, there is a difference between listening and listening well. Do you truly listen? Or are you often only hearing? When was the last time you practiced and polished your listening skills?

Why Does it Matter?

Working to be a better listener will be noticed in **all parts of your life**. Improving your listening skills improves your ability to learn, improves your relationship with the people around you, and improves your access to new and exciting opportunities.

I often talk about our journey to becoming our own best expression. Well, learning to be a better listener is a vital part of this process. You'll find that your family life, career, and social interactions will be more productive if the people around you know you are listening to them.

The Players

Jarrod and Edna Smith (the romantic relationship)

When Edna Smith sends her husband the message: "Take out the trash," she is expecting some sort of reaction from Jarrod to indicate he is listening. Whether she gets the feedback she is looking for depends on the clarity of her message and the type of listening Jarrod employs.

Jarrod bears the responsibility of listening to his wife's message, and acknowledging the consequences of applying the appropriate listening skills that their romantic relationship warrants. Should he jump up and grab the garbage immediately after being told, tell her that he'll take care of it when the game is over, or simply grunt that he hears her but the game is more important than anything she has to say? How well he reacts hinges on how well he is listening. .

Jasmine Smith and her mother, Edna (the family relationship)

When Jasmine tells her mother that she has been asked out on her first date, it is important that Edna listen for the intent behind her daughter's message. Is she asking for permission, asking for mother/daughter advice, or bragging about her new social status? It is important to the family relationship between the two that Edna listens to the message from her daughter and responds appropriately. Edna's skill in effective listening at this moment can affect Jasmine's willingness to continue coming to her mother and engaging in conversation.

Reggie Smith at college (the acquaintance relationship #1)

With only an acquaintance level relationship with his professor and other classmates, Reggie must rely more than ever on his listening skills if he is to be successful in the class. He must be attuned to the nuances of the message since his professor will be unable to customize the message just for him. Thus, the true onus of comprehension lies with Reggie. Reggie is a bright student. If he listens well, utilizing all his listening skills and applies appropriate feedback at the right times, he will be able to learn the material that his professor is lecturing about. If not...

The Smith's go out to dinner (the acquaintance relationship #2)

Both Jarrod and Jennifer, the waitress, have key listening responsibilities here. While they only share an acquaintance level

relationship, the communication between the two of them will directly affect the success of Jarrod's birthday dinner. As Jessica explains the specials, she is hoping that Jarrod is listening and coming to a conclusion about what he wants to eat. As Jarrod explains the dinner he and his family desire, he is expecting Jessica to be listening and get his order correct. The listening skills that Jessica applies here will have a direct effect on the Smiths' satisfaction with their meal, and will also affect the tip she will put in her pocket at the end of her shift.

Edna Smith at the office (the work relationship)

Edna is communicating the scope and expectations of the new project to Pam and Tom. The listening skills Pam and Tom use will determine their understanding of requirements. Appropriate and effective listening will result in everyone understanding their part in making the project successful. In fact, if Pam and Tom are listening effectively, they will be able to ask the right questions if something needs further clarification. This is an important part of appropriate feedback (which is discussed in chapter 8). Inappropriate listening, on the other hand, could result in confusion and missing the real intent of the responsibilities they are being assigned by Edna.

Jarrod Smith and his golf buddy (the friendship relationship)

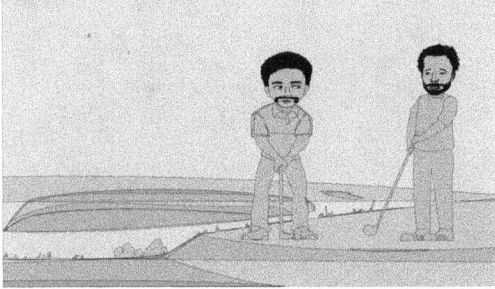

Jarrod's friend, Mike, is bearing personal information when he talks about his marital issues. The strength of their interpersonal relationship will determine the listening skills Jarrod will use. Does this conversion require Jarrod to just be a sounding board, or does he need to listen with empathy and understanding?

Chapter 3

What Is (and is not) Listening

"Listening is an art that requires attention over talent, spirit over ego, others over self." - Dean Jackson

What is Hearing?

Hearing is a **physiological process** that occurs when your ears pick up sound. It only requires that you are in range of the sound waves and that your ears and brain can absorb those sound waves. It is one of the five basic senses and occurs automatically. It doesn't even need you to be aware of it.

Hearing is a physical process that only requires that you are in range of the sound waves and that your ears and brain can absorb the sound waves.

Let's look at some examples of things which we frequently hear without actually listening to:

- The hum of the air conditioner,
- Elevator music,
- The television in the background,
- The murmur of a crowd of people

What do these things have in common? Why are these things merely heard, but not listened to? The sound is hitting our ears the same as any other message, but what inherent aspect kept these sounds from being communication and made them merely noise? The answer lies in the role of the listener.

What is Listening?

Listening is a **cognitive process**. Your brain is actually decoding and attaching meaning to the sounds. Whereas hearing is an automatic, **physiological process** listening requires you to *CHOOSE to attach meaning* to what you are hearing. In terms of the communication process, the listener is the receiver of the message. To receive the message, the receiver must be aware of the sounds or words and must translate those sounds into a message of some sort.

Listening is a psychological process that requires you to choose to attach meaning to what you are hearing

Listening requires both focus and attention to be effective. To truly listen you must not just pay attention to the story, but you

Hearing Vs. Listening

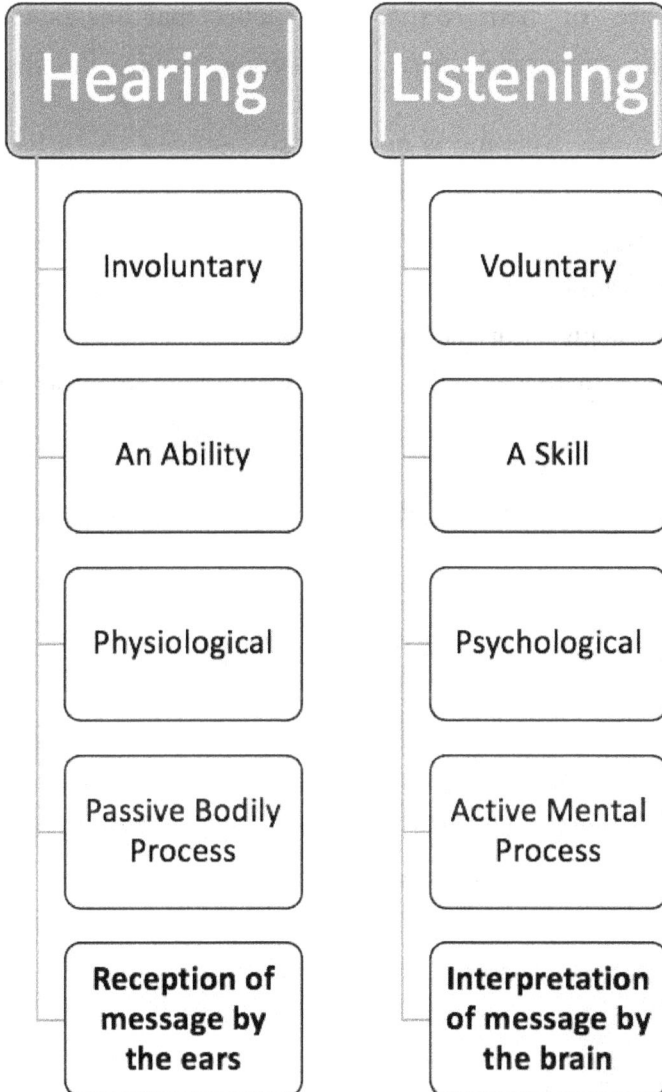

Hearing	Listening
Involuntary	Voluntary
An Ability	A Skill
Physiological	Psychological
Passive Bodily Process	Active Mental Process
Reception of message by the ears	**Interpretation of message by the brain**

should also be aware of the channel or mode of delivery. This can include both the context of the message and the environment from which the speaker is delivering the story. This means being aware of both verbal and non-verbal messages. (We'll discuss the nonverbal part of listening more in chapter 9).

As you can see, listening is not a passive process. As a listener you should be at least as engaged in the process as the speaker. We use the phrase '*active listening*' to describe this process of being fully involved in the communication exchange. To engage in active listening, you must not just hear the message, but actively seek to understand it. You must activate and utilize your mind, not just your ears.

As a listener you should be at least as engaged in the process as the speaker.

Ignoring

We would be remiss if we left this chapter without addressing ignoring. Ignoring is NOT the same as "not listening." With ignoring, the message is received and decoded, but the receiver is making a conscious decision not to acknowledge. Whereas hearing is a passive process, ignoring is an active process – just like listening.

Ignoring is NOT the same as "not listening."

As I write this, I can't help but think of the number of times I've had to raise my voice (in a loving, yet firm way of course) at one of my kids or one of the people working for me and say, "I know you can hear me! Listen to what I'm telling you." while they just keep staring at the screen in front of them. They are receiving my communication, but they are actively choosing not to respond.

In the communication process, the sender looks for feedback, any word or cue that the message was received. As the receiver, when you choose to ignore the message, you actually did listen to it. However, you are shutting the communication process down without completing the feedback part of the loop. Feedback is one of the key responsibilities of the listener. We will cover this more in chapter 8, but for now just understand that communication is a circular process. This is similar to an electrical circuit. When you break the loop, there is no power. The same holds true for communication. When a receiver breaks the loop by choosing to ignore the sender's message, the communication attempt becomes powerless.

The Players

Jarrod and Edna Smith (the romantic relationship)

When Edna calls to her husband Jarrod to take out the trash there is no doubt that he can hear her. Jarrod has normal hearing ability and Edna is not whispering. The television is at an appropriate volume that Edna's voice can easily be heard. So now the question becomes, is Jarrod really listening to her message or is he only hearing it? Will he apply the active cognitive process required to decode her message? Also, having done so, will he allow the loop to be completed with appropriate feedback, or will he choose to ignore her message? What do you think Edna's response would be in each of these three situations?

Jasmine Smith and her mother, Edna (the family relationship)

When Jasmine begins to tell her mother of her possible date, Edna is already busy with other things. Will she focus her attention on what her daughter is telling her and employ active listening? What could the consequences be if she doesn't do this, if she hears but doesn't listen? Or worse, what if she chooses to ignore her daughter because she assumes that her daughter can see that she is busy?

Reggie Smith at college (the acquaintance relationship #1)

While we will get more into the barriers to listening in Chapter 7, for right now think about the type of effort that may be required for Reggie to actively listen to his professor as opposed to merely hear him. What might happen if Reggie chooses to ignore the message? How would the professor know this has occurred with such an impersonal relationship?

The Smith's go out to dinner (the acquaintance relationship #2)

This is a situation where the consequences of not truly listening are greater for one party than the other. What could happen if Jarrod does not actively listen to Jennifer, the waitress, as she reads the specials? What about if Jennifer was not listening when Jarrod gives his order? What role does listening by either party play in the eventual success of the birthday dinner?

Edna Smith with Pam and Tom at the office (the work relationship)

As the lead on this project, Edna is trying to transmit a message to her coworkers. In this case she is the sender and her coworkers are the receivers. However, this is not the first communication that has taken place between Edna, Pam and Tom. How well Edna performed as a receiver in previous communication exchanges with Pam and Tom will play a direct role in their willingness to actively listen to her now. How has Edna's past behavior as a listener shaped the quality of the professional relationship that she shares with Pam and with Tom. If she had a history of ignoring them, do you think they would be more or less willing to employ active listening techniques to her message now? What if she historically listens actively when it is their turn to be the sender?

Jarrod Smith and Mike, his golf buddy (the friendship relationship)

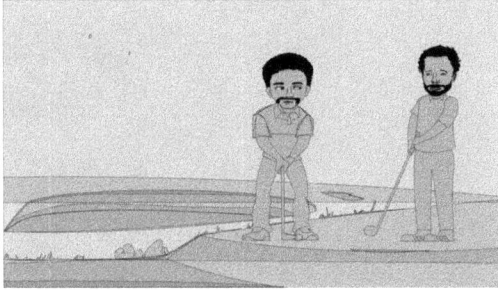

Think back on your own interactions with your friends. When you are out engaging in a sport with your friends are you just hearing them when they talk or are you really listening to what they are saying? How would Jarrod recognize that what his friend is saying is something that should be listened to? What in their relationship might affect Jarrod's decision about whether to listen to Mike's message or ignore it?

Chapter 4

Determining your Listening Style

*"YOU NEVER GET PEOPLE'S FULLER
ATTENTION THAN WHEN YOU ARE LISTENING
TO THEM." - William Feather*

How do your normally listen to people? The manner in which we generally listen to people is known as our listening style. Not everyone listens in the same way. If we did, then listening to each other would be simple and this book would be unnecessary.

The idea of listening styles is not a new concept. Over two thousand years ago Aristotle recognized that in any assembly there would be different types of listeners who would concern themselves with different aspects of a speech. In his work, _Rhetoric_, he classified listeners as assembly members who listen to judge about past events, jurymen who listen to decide about past events, and observers who listen to evaluate the speaker's skill. Now our pool of listeners of far broader than Aristotle's was. However, the concept that a person's listening style contributes to why and how they listen endures.

Each of us has a general listening style. An understanding of what your general listening style is will help you as you proceed through this book. You will be able to see how that style affects why you listen to the different people in your life, which types of listening you more easily engage in and how you can overcome the barriers that you may encounter.

Modern concepts of listening fall into one of four main listening styles:

- People-oriented listeners
- Task-oriented listeners
- Content-oriented listeners
- Time-oriented listeners

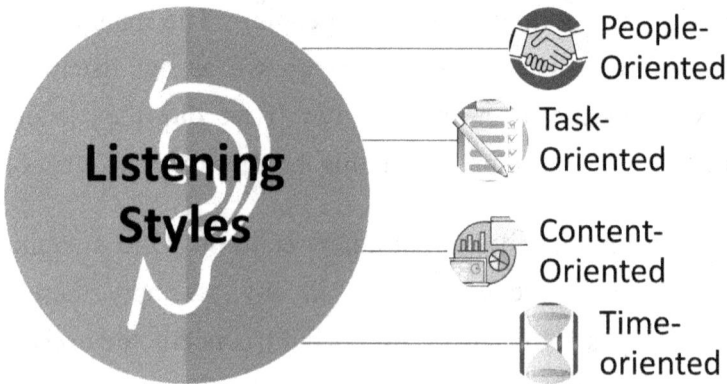

Determining your own Listening Style

So what is **your** listening style? How do you know if you are a people-oriented, task-oriented, content-oriented or time-oriented listener? And what do those different styles even mean?

Take the quiz on the next page to help you determine what your dominant listening style is. For each of the statements listed mark whether the statement is never true, seldom true, sometimes true, usually true, or always true.

For each listening style add your scores from the noted numbers. The style with the highest score indicates your dominant listening style.

Learning Styles Quiz

For each of the statements listed mark whether the statement is never true, seldom true, sometimes true, usually true, or always true.

		Never true 1 pt.	Seldom true 2 pt.	Sometimes true 3 pt.	Usually true 4 pt.	Always true 5 pt.
1	When listening to others, I focus on any errors in what's being said.					
2	When I am listening to someone I tend to smile, nod and affirm often					
3	I tend to withhold judgment about another's ideas until I have heard everything they have to say.					
4	When someone asks for my help, I wish they would give me just the facts instead of their opinions					
5	When listening to someone I tend to mentally fact check what they are telling me					
6	When people are talking to me, I tend to look at my watch or check the time					
7	When someone is asking for my help, I wish they would just tell me exactly what they want					
8	When listening to someone I often wonder where the conversation is headed					
9	When listening to others, I am mainly concerned with how they are feeling.					
10	The complement I most appreciate is you really seem to understand me					
11	I find it difficult to listen to people who take too long to get their ideas across					
12	When listening to others, I focus on understanding the feelings behind words.					
13	When listening to others, I notice contradictions in what they say.					
14	I prefer speakers who quickly get to the point					
15	I fully listen to what a person has to say before forming any opinions.					
16	When I am listening to a loved one, I wish they would remember that I have things to do.					
17	I enjoy listening to others because it allows me to connect with them.					
18	When listening to others, I consider all sides of the issue before responding.					
19	When listening to a presentation, I tend to catch errors in the speaker's logic					
20	I get frustrated when people get off topic during a conversation.					

Grading Your Quiz

For each listening style add your scores from the noted numbers. The style with the highest score indicates your dominant listening style.

People-oriented (add numbers 2, 9, 10, 12, 17)	
Task-oriented (add numbers 3, 7, 8, 15,18)	
Content-oriented (add numbers 1, 4, 5, 13, 19)	
Time-oriented (add numbers 6, 11, 14, 16, 20)	

People-Oriented

People-oriented listeners tend to be more interested in the person speaking. While they may care about the message, their usual motivation for listening centers on the speaker. For example, if you are a people-oriented listener and you were attending a workshop, you might be more interested in learning about the presenter than the presentation itself. These are the people who would ask themselves, "What does this message say about the sender? Is this person trustworthy?" A people-oriented listener wants to build relationships. They are looking for the common bond that they can share with the speaker.

Task-Oriented

Task- or action-oriented listeners tend to be more direct. They are generally more interested in finding out what the speaker wants – what is the speaker's goal. An task-oriented listener would ask themselves, "Why is this person telling me this? What do they want from me?" This person is less concerned with the speaker's motivation or how the speaker feels about their topic. If you were a task-oriented listener attending the above workshop, you might be mainly interested in finding out what the presenter is expecting you to do, buy or understand at the end. Because of this, a task-oriented listener prefers organized, error free messages.

Content-Oriented

Content-oriented listeners are more concerned with the facts themselves. They want to know if the information that the speaker passed is accurate and true. These types prefer well thought out and developed explanations that accompany a message. If you were a content-oriented listener attending a workshop you would be more concerned with whether the speaker was presenting valid information than who the speaker is or what they want. Some questions you might ask yourself include, "Does what this person is saying make sense? Is it logical? Where does he get his information?" A content-oriented listener wants to think. They enjoy complex and challenging messages where they must deliberate and make judgements. However, it is easy for a speaker to lose credibility with this listener if they don't have their facts straight.

Time-Oriented

The time-oriented listener has other places to go and things to do. They would prefer that the speaker get to the point as quickly as possible. This type of listener is often unconcerned with long and detailed explanations. "What is the point, here?" this listener asks themselves, "Could the speaker hurry up?" A time-oriented listener at the same workshop as the others would likely be checking their watch or phone or tapping their foot. They may even become distracted or leave early.

Dominant is Not All-encompasing

Now that you have determioned your dominant listening style you can begin to look at how your style matches the listening styles of those people who you interact with. Remember, though, that this is only your dominant style. We all exhibit traits of each of these styles at different times. However, once we begin to recognize these styles in ourselves and others, we are better able to intentionally nurture those positive traits and overcome those negative traits that are inherent in each style.

The Players

Jarrod and Edna Smith (the romantic relationship)

Jarrod is normally a content-oriented listener. This makes him a particularly good lawyer. He concerns himself with the facts of the message and thinks critically about the contents. He enjoys messages which provide him a mental challenge. Edna is normally an action-oriented listener. "What does this person want from me?" she wonders during many conversations. "Why are they telling me this?"

When Edna approaches Jarrod about the garbage, Jarrod is distracted and Edna is speaking. Do you think that Jarrod's listening style will help him in this situation? Will it entice him to argue over the minutia of her message and miss the point? Will he ignore the message or not listen effectively, deeming it uninteresting or unimportant? How does Edna's listening style affect how she approaches speaking? How might she accept the feedback that Jarrod may send her way?

Jasmine Smith and her mother, Edna (the family relationship)

Jasmine is normally a people-oriented listener. She normally listens to gain insight into the speaker. Her underlying goal is to build relationships. As we already mentioned, Edna is action oriented. Thus, when this conversation begins, Jasmine is trying to have a moment with her mother and Edna is... what? On one hand it is Edna's natural inclination to jump to "What does the speaker want?" However, the speaker in this conversation is someone with whom she shares a familial bond. This is her daughter. How will the nature of the relationship combine with Edna and Jasmine's natural listening styles in this conversation? How could an awareness of their listening styles help Edna and Jasmine have a more productive and enjoyable communication?

Reggie Smith at college (the acquaintance relationship #1)

Reggie is normally a people-oriented listener. Like his sister, he usually listens to learn about the speaker and build relationships. Yet a large lecture hall in a college class situation is not normally conducive to relationship building. Do you think Reggie's inclination towards people-oriented listening will be a help or a hinderance here? How would a deeper understanding of his professor help him gain a better grasp of the message? Will the distant nature of their association with the acquaintance relationship cause Reggie to become more attentive in the listening process or more distracted?

The Smith's go out to dinner (the acquaintance relationship #2)

Jessica, the waitress is normally a time-oriented listener. She has places to go and other customers to wait on. This suits her very well in her current job as a waitress. She is often able to get in, get the

customer's order, and get out of the conversation with a minimum of excess words or interactions. "Time is money" she often says. However, Jarrod, her customer at this table, is content oriented. This means his instinct is to get all of the information and analyze it. He likes to take his time and consider things carefully. How do you think this difference in listening styles will affect their conversation as Jessica tells Jarrod the specials of the day and Jarrod tells Jessica his order?

Edna Smith with Pam and Tom at the office (the work relationship)

Pam is normally a content-oriented listener. Tom is normally an action-oriented listener. Both of them are listening to Edna who is also action oriented. This is an interesting thought. Do listening styles communicate better with like listening styles? In fact, in some ways they do. A person's listening style has a direct correlation to their speaking style. You speak in a manner in which you would like to hear. Therefore, Edna would naturally tend to be more direct in her transmission of the message. Tom would find this style easier to listen to since it speaks to his natural sensibilities. Pam, on the other hand, likes to know where the facts come from. As a content-oriented listener, she is more concerned with the accuracy of the message than the purpose of the sending.

Now, just in case we thought this was a cut and dry communication case study (none of them are, by the way) consider this. Jarrod, Edna's husband of many years, is a content-oriented listener. How do you think the years of communication with someone with whom she shares a close romantic relationship might aid the communication between Edna and Pam, another content-oriented listener?

Jarrod Smith and Mike, his golf buddy (the friendship relationship)

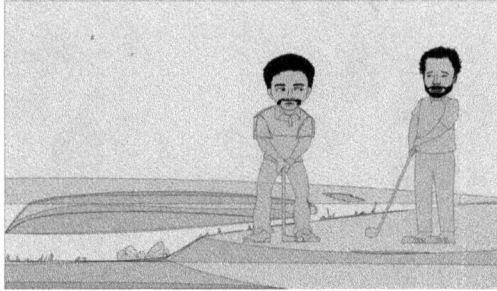

Mike is normally a time-oriented listener. However, in this instance he is primarily the one speaking. Not only that, but he is going through a personal crisis and is coming to his friend for advice and support. Thus, his delivery of his message may not stay true to his usual communication style. Jarrod, on the other hand, is still a content-oriented listener. Will this quality make it easier to listen to and help his friend? Will a preoccupation with the facts of the message make it easier or more difficult to truly empathize with Mike?

Chapter 5

WHY are you Listening?

"THE MOST BASIC AND POWERFUL WAY TO CONNECT TO ANOTHER PERSON IS TO LISTEN. JUST LISTEN. PERHAPS THE MOST IMPORTANT THING WE EVER GIVE EACH OTHER IS OUR ATTENTION. A LOVING SILENCE OFTEN HAS FAR MORE POWER TO HEAL AND TO CONNECT THAN MOST WELL-INTENTIONED WORDS." - Rachel Naomi Remen

Remember our communication model? I told you we would be coming back to this often. In this model you are the receiver. You are Mr. R.

The sender, Mrs. S, has sent her message. She has literally spoken it into existence. Now, it's all up to you. Are you prepared to receive the message that Mrs. S just sent your way?

Preparing to listen does not necessarily mean sitting in an auditorium with your pencil and paper ready to take notes. *It doesn't have to be planned or analyzed. The need to listen often just happens.* But an awareness of why you are listening, and what you hope to gain or do because of the listening, **makes you a better receiver**. This awareness can also help you overcome some of the barriers inherent to your particular listening style.

An awareness of why you are listening, and what you hope to gain or do because of the listening, makes you a better receiver.

Think about it this way: there are morning people and night people. Some of us thrive and function better in the morning and others at night. Does this mean that a night person should never get a job or set a meeting for early in the morning? Of course not. If the job or meeting is important enough, we can willingly and deliberately overcome the issues of fatigue and low energy levels that can plague us at our off times of the day. The key is that we must have a strong enough desire to do so.

The same holds true for listening. Each listening style comes with its own positives and negatives. Just because you have a particular style, though, doesn't tie you to an expected listening type. The sender is going to launch the message in their way regardless. It is up to **you** to decide what you are supposed to do with that message. This decision of yours can make or break the success of the communication. And it all starts with your why.

Are you Motivated to Listen?

If you want to be a good listener, you must **want** to be a good listener. It takes practice to nurture the skills that strengthen your listening proficiency.

*If you want to be a good listener, you must **want** to be a good listener.*

There are many reasons that we, as receivers, might WANT to listen to a message the sender is transmitting.

1. We may want to listen because we are looking to obtain information that is important to us.
2. We may want to listen because we are seeking to understand something.
3. We may want to listen for enjoyment.
4. We may want to listen to learn something.
5. We may want to listen to be courteous or polite.

6. We may want to listen to build or nurture a relationship with the sender.

7. We may want to listen to solve or prevent a problem.

8. We may want to listen so that we can become more efficient and effective at something we are doing.

9. We may want to listen to increase the sender's confidence in us.

10. We may want to listen so the sender will, in turn, listen to us.

Of course, just because we want to listen, just because we have the initial why, does not mean we are always successful at maintaining that motivation. This is where the listening-as-a-skill part comes in. One of the benefits that training and practice in listening gives us is the ability to maintain a state of active listening for longer periods of time. Remember, active listening requires focus. Holding your focus for long periods of time, or long conversations, requires sustained effort.

On the next page are some questions to ask yourself when you find your motivation to listen slipping.

8 Questions to Help Motivate you to Listen

Ask yourself each of the following questions. If you find yourself answering yes to more than a couple of the questions, it's time to **refocus your attention** and listen to what the speaker has to say.

1. Am I just pretending to listen . . . **when I should be listening?**

2. Am I seeking distractions . . . **when I should be listening?**

3. Am I criticizing the speaker . . . **when I should be listening?**

4. Have I stereotyped the topic as uninteresting . . . **when I should be listening?**

5. Have I prejudged the meaning and intent of the speaker's message . . . **when I should be listening?**

6. Am I avoiding the speaker's more difficult or complex topics . . . **when I should be listening?**

7. Am I formulating answers and follow-on questions during the speaker's presentation . . . **when I should be listening?**

8. Am I getting emotionally charged-up about some minor point the speaker made . . . **when I should be listening?**

The Players

For   each   of   our   6   situations   let's   look   at   what
the   listeners'   ***motivation   to   listen***   might   be:

Jarrod and Edna Smith (the romantic relationship)

*Below   are   some   reasons   why   Jarod   might   be   motivated
to   listen   to   Edna.   Which   of   these   do   you   think   most
likely   influence   his   choice   to   listen   to   his   wife?*

- A. *Jarrod wants to listen to be courteous or polite to Edna.*
- B. *Jarrod wants to listen in order to nurture his romantic relationship with his wife.*
- C. *Jarrod wants to listen to solve a problem or prevent a problem that would occur if his wife perceived him as ignoring her.*
- D. *Jarrod wants to listen so Edna will, later, listen to him.*

Jasmine Smith and her mother, Edna (the family relationship)

Let's look at some reasons why Edna might be motivated to listen to her daughter, Jasmine.   How would you rank these in order of which are the most likely influences in Edna's choice to actively listen to what Jasmine is saying?

> A. *Edna wants to listen because she is looking to obtain important information from Jasmine about the proposed date.*
>
> B. *Edna wants to listen because she is seeking to understand something about her daughter.*
>
> C. *Edna wants to listen in order to nurture her family relationship with her daughter.*
>
> D. *Edna wants to listen to Jasmine to solve a problem or prevent a problem.*

Reggie Smith at college (the acquaintance relationship #1)

Reggie has been actively trying to listen to his professor in class. However, he is finding his motivation to listen seems to be slipping. Think back to our list of questions to ask yourself when your motivation to listen slips. Which of the following questions would Reggie be most likely to ask himself in this situation to help him get back on track?

- A. *Am I seeking distractions **when I should be listening?***
- B. *Am I criticizing the speaker **when I should be listening?***
- C. *Have I stereotyped the topic as uninteresting **when I should be listening?***
- D. *Am I avoiding the speaker's more difficult or complex topics **when I should be listening?***
- E. *Am I formulating answers and follow-on questions during the speaker's presentation **when I should be listening?***

The Smith's go out to dinner (the acquaintance relationship #2)

Remember there are two parties in this conversation with a vested interest in listening: Jarrod and Jessica, the waitress. Look at a some of the motivations to listening listed below. Which would more likely apply to Jarrod's motivation? Which is most likely a motivation of Jessica?

> A. *I want to listen because I am looking to obtain information that is important to me.*
>
> B. *I want to listen to be courteous or polite.*
>
> C. *I want to listen to solve a problem or prevent a problem.*
>
> D. *I want to listen so that we can become more efficient and effective at something I am doing.*
>
> E. *I want to listen to increase the sender's confidence in me.*
>
> F. *I want to listen so that the sender will, in turn, listen to me.*

Edna Smith with Pam and Tom at the office (the work relationship)

Tom is struggling to listen effectively as Edna explains the parameters of the new project. Like Pam, he was initially very motivated to listen to the message Edna is sending but keeps finding his motivation slipping. Which of the following questions do you think would most benefit Tom to ask himself in this situation to help him get back on track?

> A. *Am I criticizing the speaker **when I should be listening?***

B. *Am I avoiding the speaker's more difficult or complex topics* **when I should be listening?**

C. *Am I formulating answers and follow-on questions during the speaker's presentation* **when I should be listening?**

D. *Am I getting emotionally charged-up about some minor point the speaker made* **when I should be listening?**

Jarrod Smith and Mike, his golf buddy (the friendship relationship)

Let's look at some reasons why Jarrod might be motivated to listen to his buddy, Mike.   How would you rank these in order of which are the most likely influences in Jarrod's choice to actively listen to what Mike is saying?

A. *Jarrod wants to listen for pure enjoyment.*

B. *Jarrod wants to listen to be courteous or polite to Mike.*

C. *Jarrod wants to listen in order to build or nurture the friendship relationship he has with Mike.*

D. *Jarrod wants to listen to solve a problem or prevent a problem.*

E. *Jarrod wants to listen so that the Mike will, in turn, listen to him.*

Chapter 6

5 Types of Listening

"Most people do not listen with the intent to understand. They listen with the intent to reply." - Stephen R. Covey

L et's look at our communication model again. Remember Mrs. S? She is our sender, the initiator of the communication process, the one with the message to be sent. She could have any type of reason for sending a message, but her overarching reason is to deliver meaning. Mr. R, is the receiver.

As long as he is in range, Mr. R will do one of two things:

1. He will **hear** the message, or
2. He will **listen** to the message.

If he simply hears the message, no meaning is received, and the communication cycle stops. But if he is listening, his understanding and retention will vary depending on the type of listening he engages.

Now remember that for the purposes of this book, **YOU** are Mr. R. Mrs. S is counting on you to engage in whatever type of listening is appropriate. While Mrs. S is wholly responsible for sending the message in a method that you are willing to receive, you, as Mr. R, are equally responsible for the actual act of listening. You are the R-man! If you don't do your part, then the communication will be unsuccessful.

> ***While the sender is wholly responsible for sending the message in a method that you are willing to receive, you, as the reciever, are equally responsible for the actual act of listening.***

In my certification training to become a Stephens Minister we spent a significant amount of time working on the idea that we were there to listen to problems not to solve them. This was a challenge for me because my natural inclination is that of a "fixer" not a "nurturer". As we worked through the practices and scenarios my mind would instantly go to all the ways in which the care receiver could solve or "fix" their issue. This made it more difficult for me to be an effective caregiver. I had to intentionally practice listening to empathize as opposed to listening to decode or to fix. Luckily, all this practice was precisely the point of the months-long Stephens minister training. It helped me hone my skills in the **types of listening needed** for people who were going through a crisis. You see, it's not enough to just actively listen. To be a good listener you need to understand what kind of listening you should use depending on the situation you are in.

> ### _To be a good listener you need to understand what kind of listening you should use depending on the situation you are in._

To help you to fulfill your duties as a great and powerful "R-Man", you should understand the different types of listening, along with their advantages in different situations. These listening types include:

- Appreciative listening
- Discriminative listening
- Comprehensive listening
- Emphatic listening
- Critical listening

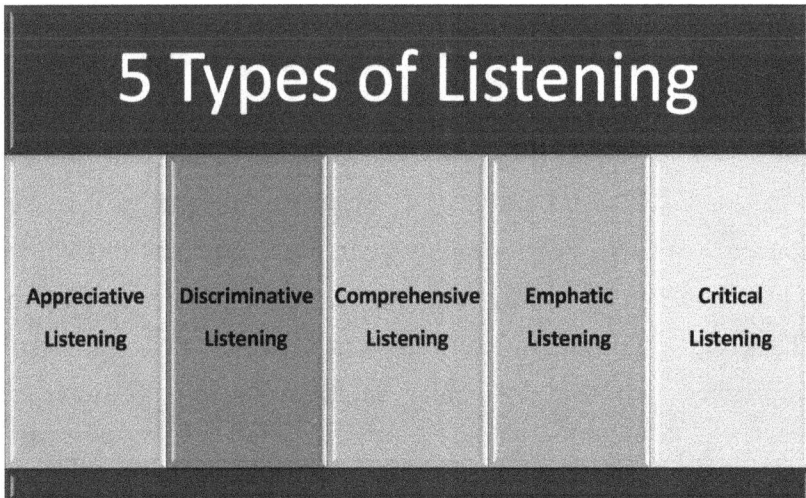

5 Types of Listening

| Appreciative Listening | Discriminative Listening | Comprehensive Listening | Emphatic Listening | Critical Listening |

Decoding the 5 types

Appreciative Listening

Appreciative   listening   is   for   your   enjoyment.
It   doesn't   require   a   significant   amount   of   focus,
but   it   also   does   not   result   in   significant   retention.

This could also be called **"social listening."** You could be sitting
on the bleachers at your son's little league game listening to the
mother of another player telling you about the day her child was the
best hitter on the team. The big difference between appreciative
listening and just hearing is that you are accepting meaning from
Mrs. S, and are forming visions, ideas, or responses because of them.

> *__The big difference between appreciative listening and just hearing__*
> *__is that you are accepting meaning and are forming visions, ideas, or__*
> *__responses because of them.__*

These visions, ideas or responses that you form, while both basic
and general, are still suited to the type of message that Mrs. S is
sending. For example, if the message is positive, you may smile and
nod in response. If the message is negative, you may affect a look
of concern. We will get more into appropriate feedback in Chapter 8.
The key here, though, is that your responses in appreciative listening
are basic and minimal. While you want to listen enough to respond
appropriately you are not really invested in the message itself.

Appreciative listening is something you could possibly employ with acquaintances as opposed to friends or family relationships. When you think about your *why*, appreciative listening would fall into the realm of listening to be polite or for enjoyment as opposed to actually needing to get usable information from the message. For appreciative listening, simply acquiring the message is enough.

Discriminative Listening

Discriminative listening requires more effort because you are listening to the meaning of the message. Your goal is to understand Mrs. S. **You listen to her words, pay attention to her nonverbal cues, and form opinions on what you see and hear.**

You use discriminative listening when your mechanic explains what that "thump thump" coming from your car means. Nonverbals like rolling his eyes, wringing his hands, or winking to another mechanic, may add a different meaning to his verbal diagnosis of "nothing wrong."

You could also use this type of listening in a room with a group of people speaking a language you don't know. Without understanding a word being said, you gain a lot of clues just from the inflections and gestures accompanying the words. By trying to attach meaning to the unfamiliar words, volume, and pitch, you are also watching facial expressions and body movement. You are listening discriminatively.

Discriminative listening may be used when someone is trying to explain something to you that you need to understand. This could be directions, explanations, or descriptions. The point to discriminative listening lies in the fact that it's the comprehension, the true understanding of their message, not just the reception that is important.

When you use discriminative listening your goal should be more than just being nice or sociable. You should have a selfish motive as well. You are invested in the message and actively want to decipher it. You give the sender your attention and listen with your ears and your eyes.

Remember, it's the meaning of the message that is important to you when you use discriminative listening. It is not the sender, or the channel of transmission, or even the emotional relationships. The key to discriminative listening is comprehension, not just acquisition.

The key to discriminative listening is comprehension, not just acquisition.

Comprehensive Listening

Comprehensive listening attempts to not only understand Mrs. S's message, **but also to learn from or remember what she is communicating**.

The previous two types of listening focused simply on decoding meaning. You may or may not remember the details later but understood the meaning of what was being communicated. When you move into comprehensive listening, though, you are intending to remember the meaning behind the message.

__When you move into comprehensive listening you are intending to__
__remember the meaning behind the message.__

As Mr. R, you engage your comprehensive listening skills when your pharmacist is explaining how your new meds should be taken. A parent listens to remember what his teen-age daughter says she will be doing on her evening out with friends. You listen to your relative telling you how to get to their new house.

This is the next step up from discriminative listening. It is important for you to understand the true meaning of the message, yes, but it is also important for you to store that message in your long-term memory. You know that you will be required to recall that message later. When that happens, it will be important that the message you recall is the same as the original message the sender communicated. This act of transferring a message to memory requires deeper concentration and the firing of other parts of your brain.

Remember, for comprehensive listening you don't just want to hear it (like in Appreciative listening), you don't just want to understand it (like in Discriminative listening), but you want to **remember the message** as well.

Emphatic Listening

Emphatic listening attempts to not only understand the message, but to understand **how Mrs. S feels about what she is saying**.

Counselors, therapists, and clergy are obvious examples of people who must be skilled in emphatic listening. But if your Mrs. S is a friend or colleague needing a sounding board, you'll want to be able to listen appropriately. Have you ever poured your heart out to a significant person in your life, only to realize they were in social listening mode? You may as well have been talking to the mirror.

Emphatic listening leans heavier than the previous types on the relationship between the sender and the receiver. Unless you're in the type of profession where you regularly utilize this type of listening, most of us save emphatic listening for people with whom we share a closer bond. This may be your close friends and family members and people with whom you share a romantic relationship.

The key to emphatic listening is the idea that you care about how the other person feels about their message, not just the content of the message. You might pay closer attention to the nonverbal cues that Mrs. S is giving. You would also alter your feedback to give the idea that you don't just understand the message, but you understand the person as well, and you care about them.

The key to emphatic listening is the idea that you care about how the other person feels about their message, not just the content of the message.

When practicing emphatic listening, you may respond with phrases such as "How did that make you feel?" or "That must have been awfully hard for you." This is different from a comprehensive listening response such as "Could you repeat that, more slowly?"

Your feedback will focus on the sender's reaction to their own message. This is because with this type of listening the state of the sender is equal in importance to you as the content of the message.

Sometimes I get stuck in emphatic listening when it is not appropriate. A speaker can go into a personal experience example to back up a point, and I get so wrapped up in the *feelings* that I forget to listen to the *message*. Emphatic listening may be difficult for some types of people, but those who easily slip into this mode, need to be able to step back into the style of listening to fit the speaker's purpose.

Critical Listening

Critical listening requires you to **hear, understand, evaluate and judge** a message. *This is the most demanding form of listening because of the focus and concentration required.* When employing critical listening you must not only decode verbal and nonverbal messages, but you must also evaluate Mrs. S's credibility and honesty, while analyzing the message. With this type of listening you are trying to determine if you believe the message and if it is important enough to remember.

When employing critical listening you must not only decode verbal and nonverbal messages, but you must also evaluate the sender's credibility and honesty, while analyzing the message.

You might use your critical listening skills when listening to a salesman trying to earn a commission through you. You would use this with a politician trying to earn your vote. If Mrs. S is a high school teacher or college professor, she is counting on her students being able use their critical listening skills.

Critical listening requires the listener to be able to evaluate and judge both the sender and the message without being judgmental.   As we will talk more about later, personal bias is considered one of the main barriers to listening.   To successfully employ critical listening, Mr. R, the receiver — **YOU** — must be able to look past the implicit bias, to overcome the barriers that keep you from understanding Mrs. S and her message.

So how do you accomplish this? When you employ critical listening, you need to evaluate both the situation and the claims in the message. You are looking to see if there is support for the validity of the message. Like a judge weighing the facts in a case, you are making the decision for yourself whether you will believe the message that the sender transmits.

How to Choose your Listening Type

I remember one supervisor I had many years ago who was always in the time-oriented style of listening.   I would go into his office to explain a situation, looking for some critical listening on his part.   But the only responses I could get out of him were, "What's the bottom line," or "What's the point here?"

Because he was not able to listen in a way that I needed, I learned to never go to him for advice or approval on situations. When choosing your listening style, you need to think not only of what you want to get out of the communications, but also at what style the speaker *needs* you to use.

> *When choosing your listening style, you need to think not only of what you want to get out of the communications, but also at what style the speaker needs you to use.*

It's not enough just to know what the listening types are. You should be aware of what type of listening you should be doing for the situation. To help you determine the best listening type for your situation ask yourself the following questions:

1. Do I really care about the message or am I just being **sociable**?

   - If you are listening to be sociable, use **Appreciative Listening**

2. Do I need to **understand** what is being communicated?

   - If so, use **Discriminative Listening**

3. Will I need to **remember** what is being communicated later?

   - If so, use **Comprehensive Listening**

4. Am I concerned about the **emotional state** of the sender or do we share an **emotional connection**?

   - If so, use **Emphatic Listening**

5. Will I need to **evaluate** and make a **judgement** based on the message being communicated?

   - If so, use **Critical Listening**

Listening TYPE Flowchart

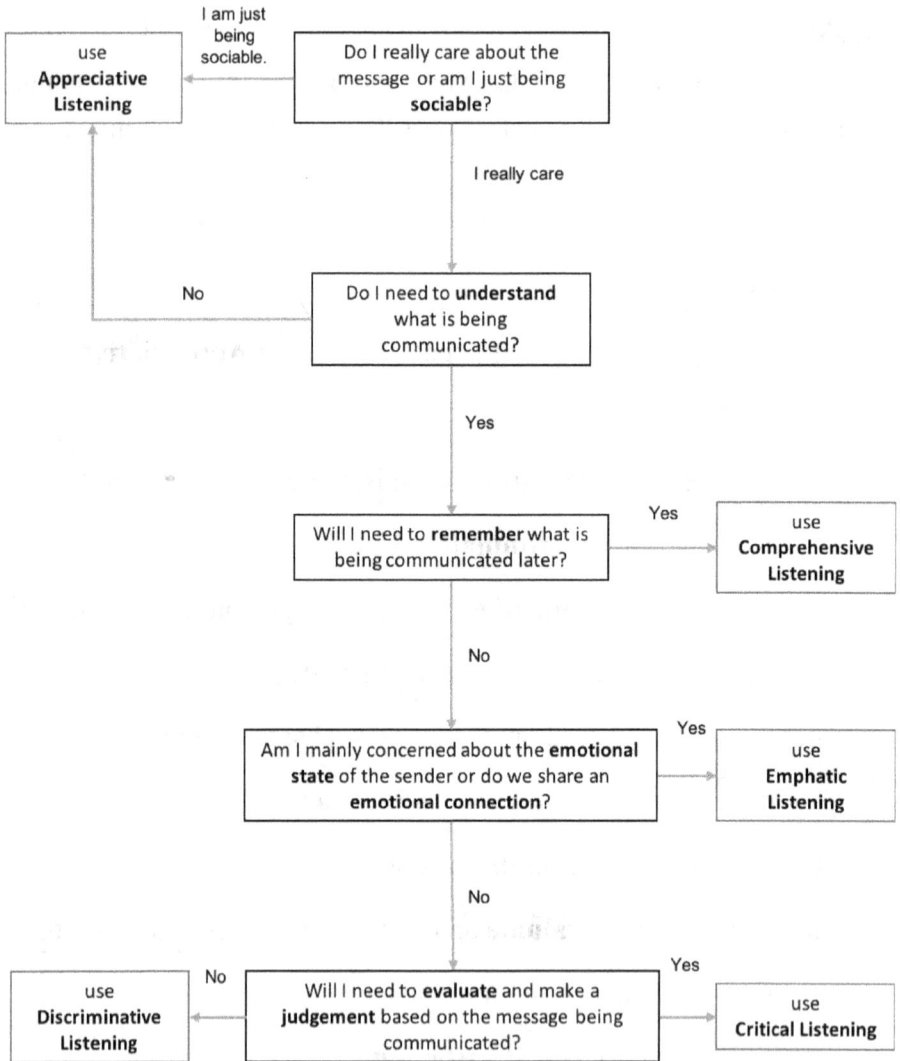

```
                            I am just
                             being
┌──────────────┐           sociable.  ┌──────────────────────┐
│     use      │ ◄──────────────────── │ Do I really care about the │
│ Appreciative │                       │  message or am I just being │
│  Listening   │                       │        sociable?           │
└──────────────┘                       └──────────────────────┘
        ▲                                        │
        │                                   I really care
        │                                        │
        │                                        ▼
        │              ┌──────────────────────┐
        │      No      │ Do I need to understand │
        └───────────── │    what is being       │
                       │    communicated?       │
                       └──────────────────────┘
                                 │
                                Yes
                                 │
                                 ▼
                       ┌──────────────────────┐   Yes   ┌──────────────┐
                       │ Will I need to remember what is │────────►│     use      │
                       │  being communicated later?      │         │ Comprehensive │
                       └──────────────────────┘         │  Listening   │
                                 │                       └──────────────┘
                                 No
                                 │
                                 ▼
                       ┌──────────────────────┐   Yes   ┌──────────────┐
                       │ Am I mainly concerned about the emotional │──►│     use      │
                       │ state of the sender or do we share an     │   │   Emphatic   │
                       │      emotional connection?                │   │  Listening   │
                       └──────────────────────┘         └──────────────┘
                                 │
                                 No
                                 │
                                 ▼
┌──────────────┐   No   ┌──────────────────────┐   Yes   ┌──────────────┐
│     use      │◄────── │ Will I need to evaluate and make a │──────►│     use      │
│Discriminative│        │ judgement based on the message being │     │Critical Listening│
│  Listening   │        │       communicated?                  │     └──────────────┘
└──────────────┘        └──────────────────────┘
```

The Players

Let's look at our 6 situations again. As we do examine what type of listening the receiver should engage in to facilitate the best possible communication experience.

Jarrod and Edna Smith (the romantic relationship)

Edna Smith wants the garbage taken out. However, Jarrod is right in the middle of the big game. In the last chapter we looked at reasons why Jarrod might be compelled to listen to his wife. If he were wanting to build a deeper relationship or prevent future problems what kind of listening should he employ. Is he invested in the message? Is it important that he understand what Edna wants him to do? Will he need to remember the instructions later? How important do you think Edna's emotions concerning the trash are to her husband?

Jasmine Smith and her mother, Edna (the family relationship)

Imagine you are Edna Smith. Your daughter is telling you all about her would-be date and needs your permission. What kind of listening would you want use here? Is this your opportunity to find out about and make a judgement on this boy who wants to date your daughter? Perhaps Jasmine is telling you about where they will be going on their date. This might be important information to remember later if she is not back by curfew. Even though you are busy and there are several barriers present (which we will talk about next chapter) it is important that you utilize more than simple appreciative listening.

Reggie Smith at college (the acquaintance relationship #1)

Reggie Smith is at a disadvantage. He doesn't have the type of relationship with his professor that will lend itself to more involved types of listening. Yet, the message that his professor is sending is

very important to Reggie if he wants a good grade in the class. What type of listening do you think would suit him best here? Would the type of listening be different if this class were a subject that came easy to Reggie? What if this class were a difficult subject for him?

The Smith's go out to dinner (the acquaintance relationship #2)

Remember, there are two sides to the listening coin in this scenario. We have Jarrod as the listener and then we have Jessica as the listener. Does the type of listening Jarrod needs to use while Jessica is reading the specials the same type of listening that Jessica should use when Jarrod is telling her his order? Would the type of listening Jarrod should employ be different if he already knows upon entering the restaurant what he wants to order? What if he has never been to the restaurant before?

Edna Smith with Pam and Tom at the office (the work relationship)

Edna is trying to explain specifics of the project to Pam and Tom. As the sender, her goal is to make sure that her coworkers understand what they need to do to successfully complete the project. However, depending on the "why's" that Pam and Tom have, the type of listening that they use could be very different from the type that should be warranted. On one hand they could employ comprehensive listening. Remember this is where they seek to both understand and remember the message. This would be important when they get back to their own desks or offices so that they can remember how to do their part of the project. However, based on what they know about Edna they may, in fact, be employing critical listening. How do you think their perception of Edna would affect their comprehension of the message that she is sending?

Jarrod Smith and Mike, his golf buddy (the friendship relationship)

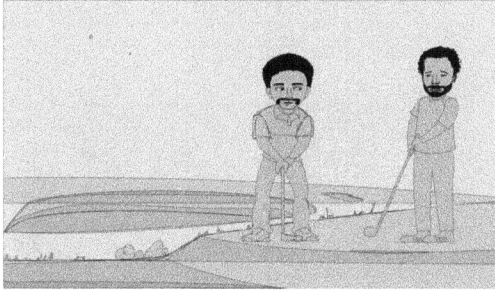

How good of friends do you think that Jarrod and Mike are?   Are they the type of friends who hang out for the enjoyment of it but otherwise keep things on the surface?   Or are they the type of friends that bare their souls to each other and keep each other's confidences?

Think about the different why's we mentioned in the last chapter for Jarrod in this scenario.   What kind of listening would Jarrod employ if he is being polite to his friend, but really just wants to play golf?   What kind of listening would he employ if he knew that Mike's wife and Edna were best friends?

Here's a question for you.   What kind of listening do you think that Mike is hoping his friend is using?   What kind of listening would you want your friends to use if you were in Mike's shoes?

Chapter 7

Barriers to Effective Listening

"NOISE POLLUTION IS A RELATIVE THING.
IN A CITY, IT'S A JET PLANE TAKING
OFF. IN A MONASTERY, IT'S A PEN
THAT SCRATCHES." - Robert Orben

I have a brother that is two years older than me. However due to a nomadic, military upbringing it wasn't until high school that I walked into my first class with a teacher that had also been his teacher. At the time I was unprepared with how the fact that my brother had also had this teacher was going to affect my experience with her class. You see, I entered the class with a wealth of information and gossip from my brother about the teacher, her teaching style, and the nature of the class. My brother had a very distinct personality back then and the teacher started the year with the expectation of another one of *those* siblings in her class. For the first several weeks of class our psychological barriers and personal biases got in the way of true communication and made learning difficult. It was only through concerted effort on both sides that we were able to overcome the noise and barriers between us.

Barriers are things that get in the way. These can also be called noise. Listening, as with any other skill, has normal, expected hinderances to achieving full success. A quarterback may have a stiff shoulder hindering the strength of his throw. The tuba player may have a cold that is interfering with her ability to take deep enough breaths to play a long note. With listening, barriers are reasons why Mr. R is less than successful.

Barriers are things that get in the way. These can also be called noise.

Let's take a look at our communication model. Remember this?

Notice that the barriers are present between Mrs. S and Mr. R in both directions of the process. This means that they exist and get in the way of successful communication both for the sender and the receiver. However, while barriers can initiate at any point in the process, it is important to note that barriers **interfere with the interpretation of the message by the receiver.** In short, while the cause of the barrier may lie with Mrs. S or Mr. R, the effects of the barrier will be experienced by Mr. R. This is why it is so important that you, the receiver, are aware of the barriers that exist and take what steps you can to overcome them.

Barriers interfere with the interpretation of the message by the receiver

There are many different factors that can act as barriers to listening. These fall into four major categories:

- Physical Barriers
- Psychological Barriers
- Semantic Barriers
- Biases

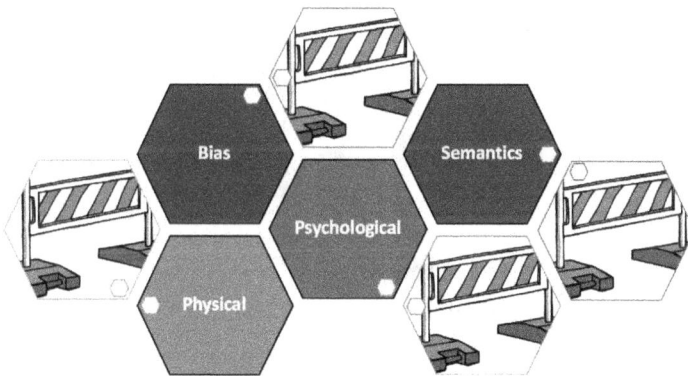

4 Types of Barriers to Listening

Physical Barriers

Physical barriers are those types of noise that are direct environmental interferences. Physical barriers can be environmental or physiological.

Environmental barriers are items in the environment that are distracting. This could be audible stimuli such as the sound of the air conditioner or the chatter of the group at the next table. It could be visual – a flickering light overhead or distracting movement on the television. Perhaps you are having a conversation over a meal and the smells and tastes of the food are distracting you from the message. Any sort of noisy equipment, visual interferences, and personal distractions (fatigue or illness) can make it hard for a listener to focus in on the sounds coming from the speaker. All of these make up physical barriers.

Environmental barriers are items in the environment that are distracting.

Physical barriers also include **physiological barriers**. These are the physical things going on with our body that may be distracting. Think about how hard it is to pay attention to a conversation when you have a headache. Have you noticed how hard it is to listen to a speaker when your foot falls asleep? If you are anything like me, having your foot fall asleep in any situation is the absolute worst. For me, trying to follow a conversation, especially one that requires comprehensive or critical listening, can be incredibly difficult. The presence of physiological barriers requires an extra concentration effort on your part to overcome.

Physiological barriers are the physical things going on with our body that may be distracting.

Psychological Barriers

Psychological barriers are the things going on in the listener's mind that interfere with the interpretation of the message. Events at work, conditions at home, problems with finances hinder one's ability to concentrate on the message. Consider all the many small things that we often think about when we should be listening. Worry, stress, anxiety – those small nagging thoughts go by many names. However, the effect is the same. Distraction. Psychological barriers are the distractions in our minds that keep us from focusing on the sender's message.

Semantic Barriers

Semantics is the study of the meanings of words and phrases. Semantic barriers exist when the sender uses words that the receiver doesn't understand. Words or phrases with more than one meaning, jargon, and organizational acronyms can make a sender's message undecipherable to a receiver.

__Semantic barriers exist when the sender uses words that the receiver doesn't understand.__

Barriers of semantics often are experienced in technical conversations and in conversations with non-native language speakers. The sender makes the assumption that the listener has the same background as it pertains to vocabulary as they do. Thus, they throw out words and phrases that are specific to the type of message that they are sending.

The problem comes, however, when the listener does not have the assumed experience or knowledge base. In this case, the actual words themselves may carry a different meaning to Mr. R than intended.

Semantic barriers are something my family had to contend with. My mother spent 20 years in the Air Force. My grandfather was a civilian employee of the Army. When my whole family would get together, military acronyms came spewing out of my grandpa's and mom's mouths. How often my aunts and uncles would find reasons to leave the room. One might have thought they were being polite and giving grandpa and mom some one-on-one time. But in reality, they felt like outsiders because they couldn't understand all the jargon in the conversations.

Biases

Biases are differences in personal feelings and beliefs about such things as age, race, gender, and personal appearance that can alter the receiver's decoding of the message. A biased Mr. R believes "I don't have to listen to Mrs. S's message because I already know what I think."

There are two types of biases a listener can hold which affect the interpretation of the message. First, Mr. R could be biased against the topic. Perhaps you're listening to a speech you've heard before or the speaker is sending a message about a topic that you are familiar with. When a listener has prior knowledge and opinions about a topic it can make it difficult to consider new information, especially if it conflicts with what a listener believes they know.

The other type of bias is related to what the listener thinks about the speaker themselves. If a listener has strong negative feelings about the sender, it colors their opinion of the message. Perhaps they believe the speaker is untrustworthy or unknowledgeable. If this is the case, the Mr. R may be less inclined to objectively listen to the message Mrs. S is trying to send him.

Whatever types of biases exist, they carry the potential of poisoning the listener's interpretation of the message. The receiver doesn't hear the true message. Instead they only hear what they want to hear.

I'll admit here for everyone to know: I am not free of personal biases and have to make some special effort to concentrate on some speaker's' messages to overcome my personal barriers. My bias? In danger of offending someone, please forgive me here. I have great difficulty listening to public speakers who mangle their words with poor grammar. Nitpicky? Yes. But it does get in my way since I spend more time mentally correcting sentences rather than listening to the message.

So, what might your biases be? Identify them honestly (you don't have to publish them in a book as I just did). But be aware of them when you get into a situation where they will become a barrier to effective listening. The speaker probably has something worth listening to despite your preconceived stereotyping.

Overcoming Barriers

I have great news! The 4 barriers to effective listening are not insurmountable. Just like intentional action can help us overcome the barriers in life, intentional action can help us overcome the barriers to successful communication. We can use the 3 C's of Overcoming Barriers to effective listening. These 3 C's are:

1. Create an awareness of the barriers
2. Clear the channel of pragmatic problems
3. Concentrate despite the barriers

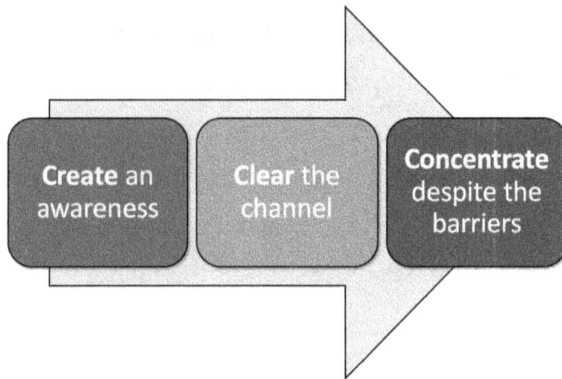

Create an Awareness of the Barriers

The first way to combat listening barriers is to create an awareness of the barriers themselves. This may seem simple and self-explanatory, yet it is often the most difficult step to take. Creating an awareness of your barriers involves a measure of self-reflection. Ask yourself the following questions:

- Am I fully focused on the sender of the message or am I distracted?

- Are there things in the environment that are distracting me?
- Am I worried, stressed or anxious? Are my thoughts straying from the speaker and her message?
- How do I feel about the speaker? Is it coloring how I am interpreting the message?
- How do I feel about the topic? Is it coloring how I am interpreting the message?
- Do I understand the words the speaker is using? Do I know what they mean?

Clear the channel of pragmatic problems

A pragmatic problem relates matters of fact and practical affairs. Basically, clearing the channel of pragmatic problems involves fixing what you can fix. Especially when it comes to the physical barriers to listening there are often several actions you can take to lessen your distractions. Are you cold? Put on a jacket or sweater. Do you tend to feel sleepy when you are trying to listen to someone? Make sure you are getting an adequate amount of sleep at night. Often one of the best things, that a listener can do to clear the channel is to make sure they are facing the speaker and looking at them. This puts the attention of both your eyes and ears on the same topic. It also helps you pay more attention to nonverbal cues which is a key component to active listening. Remember, nonverbal cues can often make the difference between accurate and faulty understanding of the true message (nonverbal cues are discussed in more detail in Chapter 9). The key here is to fix those distractions that are in your power to fix.

Concentrate despite the barriers

Once you have identified your barriers and cleared the ones that can be cleared the third step is to concentrate. This one, we know, can be easier said than done. How do you concentrate when you are distracted? How do you focus on the speaker when you have physical, psychological, and semantic barriers and noise standing between you and the true message the speaker is sending? You concentrate. You actively focus and refocus your attention on the speaker and what the speaker is saying. Here are a few tactics you can use when you find your focus slipping:

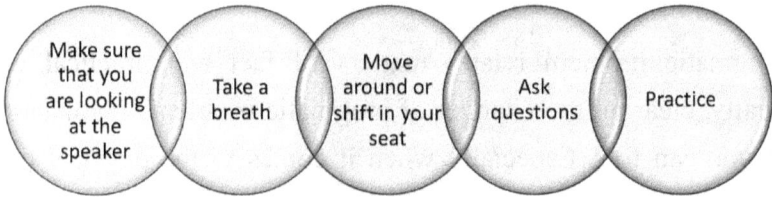

Make sure that you are looking at the speaker | Take a breath | Move around or shift in your seat | Ask questions | Practice

1. **Make sure that you are looking at the speaker**. We mentioned this a few minutes ago when we were talking about clearing the channels, but the same practice is applicable here to. Often when our focus wavers, our eyes follow. Look back to the sender of the message.
2. **Take a breath**. Breathing has a wonderful ability to ground us and bring us back into an awareness of ourselves. When you take a deep breath it's like you are grabbing hold of your attention and moving it back to where you want it to be.
3. **Move around or shift in your seat**. Physical movement wakes up our muscles, gets our blood pumping and oxygen

moving. Even small movements can give your body and brain the jolt they need to refocus on the task at hand which is listening to Mrs. S.

4. **Ask questions**. When you are asking questions and giving appropriate feedback you are becoming an active participant in the conversation. You are investing in the topic and in the communication exchange. Every time you open your mouth to ask a question or to give some feedback you are plugging back into the sender and the sender's message.

5. **Practice.** Many of us have heard the phrase "Fake it 'til you make it" or something similar. Your brain is a muscle. Your ability to concentrate and focus, to overcome the barriers to listening, is a direct use of your brain muscle. So, how do we grow a muscle? We feed it and we use it. Your ability to listen effectively will only improve with use. You need to practice focusing and actively listening. The more you do it, the easier it will get.

Your brain is a muscle. Your ability to concentrate and focus, to overcome the barriers to listening, is a direct use of your brain muscle

The Players

So back to our 6 situations. For each one let's look at what different barriers might exist that could get in the way of them receiving the true meaning of the message.

Jarrod and Edna Smith (the romantic relationship)

Think about the situation with Jarrod and his wife Edna. Jarrod has several things working against him and his ability to listen to Edna. First, since he is watching and is engaged in the television, he is not looking at her. He has both physical barriers with the sounds and sights of the game, but also psychological ones. Is he thinking about his wife or the trash at this moment? Or is he thinking about football? What are some actions that Jarrod might take to address some of his barriers?

Jasmine Smith and her mother, Edna (the family relationship)

Jasmine really wants to pass a message to her mother. What kinds of barriers do you think exist that may be keeping Edna from really listening to her daughter's message? Since she just got home from

work, she may be feeling physical barriers like fatigue or she may have a headache. She is starting to cook dinner so she may have the sights, smells and sounds of cooking to distract her. Perhaps she is still dealing with psychological noise from her day at work. This could be leaving her distracted. Also, any parent who has ever had a conversation with a child or teenager knows that there may be words and phrases that our children use that are completely foreign to us. Teenage slang is a legitimate semantic barrier in a conversation with parents. What other barriers to communication do you think exist here? What could Edna do to lessen or address these barriers?

Reggie Smith at college (the acquaintance relationship #1)

Poor Reggie has quite a few barriers working against him here. He is really going to have to use all his tricks in his 4 C's bag to help him overcome these. First, he is in a crowded classroom and not in the front row. This means there is bound to be an increased amount of visual and auditory stimuli to distract him. He may have a preconceived bias against his instructor based upon what he may have heard about the instructor's knowledge level or teaching style. As a college student Reggie may have any number of worries and anxieties causing a psychological barrier. Finally, depending on what kind of class it is, there may be any number of words that

the professor uses that Reggie is not familiar with. Knowing this may be the case, what are some things that Reggie could have done before coming to class to help clear the channel for himself once he got there? What are some ways that Reggie could help himself concentrate despite the barriers now that he is in the class?

The Smith's go out to dinner (the acquaintance relationship #2)

So, let's focus for a moment here on Jessica, the waitress. She is trying to listen to the Smiths' order. It is important for her to get this right. She could be very invested, and yet have nearly insurmountable barriers working against her. Perhaps she is nearing the end of an eight-hour shift. She is tired and her feet hurt. She knows if she doesn't get off on time she will be late to pick up her son from the sitter. However, she needs the extra tip she is hoping to get from the Smiths because rent is coming due. The restaurant is crowded and noisy. A few tables away a baby is crying.

What are the different barriers that exist for Jessica as she is trying to listen to Jarrod Smith give his order? What are some things that she can do to help her focus and listen effectively?

Edna Smith with Pam and Tom at the office (the work relationship)

Pam and Tom are in the same room, having the same conversation with the same person. However, the barriers each is experiencing as they try to listen to Edna are quite different.

Secretly, Pam does not think Edna is competent to lead this project. She should have been chosen as the project lead. While it is important to all three of them that the project be successful, Pam knows that Edna doesn't have the experience to lead a project of this size. How will this bias affect Pam's desire and ability to listen effectively to Edna. Since Pam also has a vested interest in the success of the project, what can she do to combat this bias so that she can accurately receive the messages that Edna is trying to send?

Tom on the other hand was thrilled that Edna was chosen as the project lead. He has always respected her competence in the workplace. He is young and new at the company and is excited to get to work on this project with both Edna and Pam. Tom and his wife just had a new baby, though, and Tom has only been getting a couple of hours a sleep each night. To top it off, this new project is coming with a whole list of technical terms and acronyms that Tom has never heard of. What types of barriers exist for Tom? What are some things that he can do to make sure that he is getting the full and accurate message that Edna is sending?

Jarrod Smith and Mike, his golf buddy (the friendship relationship)

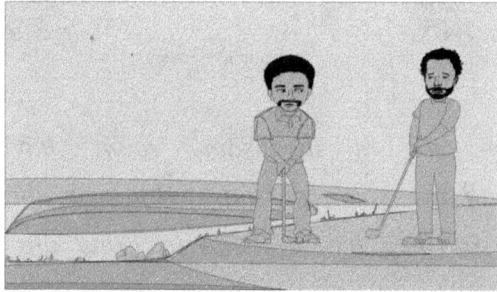

It is a beautiful day. The sun is shining; it is neither too hot nor too cold. It is the perfect day for a game of golf. Jarrod has been waiting all week for the chance to hit some balls with his friend. However, it seems that his friend wants to do more talking and less golfing. Mike has been having some problems in his marriage and has chosen today to come to his friend for help and advice. What kind of barriers do you think Jarrod is experiencing while trying to actively listen to Mike? What kinds of physical barriers can exist on a beautiful day? What types of psychological barriers and biases might Jarrod hold? Do you think any semantic barriers might exist in this conversation? And what actions can Jarrod take here to ensure that he is listening in the way that Mike needs him to?

Chapter 8

Feedback

"WE ALL NEED PEOPLE WHO WILL GIVE US FEEDBACK.
THAT'S HOW WE IMPROVE" - Bill Gates

Hopefully, you've noticed in our communication model that between Mrs. S and Mr. R there is also a label called **Feedback.** Feedback has been mentioned several times throughout this book. In fact, a book on how to become a better listener would be sadly incomplete without a discussion of feedback.

What is Feedback

Feedback is an integral part of the communication process. **It is Mr. R's response to what Mrs. S is saying.** Feedback tells Mrs. S whether Mr. R is understanding her message. And it provides her information on what Mr. R's emotional reaction to the message might be, and whether she needs to modify her delivery method. Once the sender receives the feedback from the listener, she can modify her strategy for sending or resending messages to suit. Without this piece, though, the sender is basically just giving a monologue.

> **_Feedback is the receiver's response to what the sender is saying._**

Just like all the other components of listening, though, giving feedback is a skill. If, as a listener, we don't pay adequate attention to how we give feedback, and we don't practice the giving of appropriate feedback, that skill can become rusty. Let's take a look at some of the characteristics that make up this component of communication we call feedback.

Characteristics of Feedback

Feedback may be verbal or non-verbal

Verbal feedback allows the receiver to voice his thoughts about the message. Verbal feedback can take the form of questions and statements. It can also just be sounds or short utterances. "I see" or "Uh-huh" are both types of verbal feedback that may be perfectly appropriate depending on the type of listening that we are employing.

Remember when we talked about types of listening back in chapter 5? Well, the verbal or non-verbal type of feedback you should employ has a direct correlation with the type of listening that you are undertaking.

Non-verbal feedback is the receiver's reaction through the facial expressions, posture, and gestures. A nod, a frown, arms crossed, a roll of the eyes tells the sender a lot. We will cover this a bit more in the next chapter. For now, it's important to note that what you are NOT saying is just as valid of feedback as the words and sounds that come out of your mouth.

Feedback can be positive or negative.

Positive feedback tells the sender that the message is understood and/or accepted. The receiver's smile and nod give affirmation to the sender. This tells the sender that the way she was delivering the message was effective and that she should continue in the same way. This could also tell the sender that you are pleased with the information contained in the message.

Negative feedback, on the other hand, could tell the sender that she needs to alter her manner of communication. The receiver's frown and scrunched eyebrows may indicate he is either confused or disagrees with the message. As a receiver, this is where you may ask clarifying questions. All these things tell the sender that there is a break in the communication pathway. One of the barriers is interfering with the communication and the sender may need to rethink how they are transmitting the message.

Feedback can be natural or deliberate.

Natural feedback is the immediate, spontaneous reaction to the message. It is the most honest feedback. Much of the natural feedback given by the receiver comes in the form of nonverbal cues. Nodding, smiling, or yawning are all different types of natural feedback that the sender can then interpret in different ways.

Deliberate feedback is thought about and calculated prior to sending. The receiver thinks about the message and decides what his reaction should be. This is often the preferred method of feedback. You, as the listener, take control of the type and manner of feedback that you want to send. This might be especially true if the sender's reaction to your feedback is important to you. Think about the different types of relationships we discussed at the beginning of the book. Depending on your relationship with the Mrs. S, you may have differing levels of desire to have your feedback interpreted in a positive manner. The only way to control the reception of your feedback is to control what kind of feedback you send through deliberate action.

Feedback can be immediate or delayed

Immediate feedback occurs when the receiver communicates right away whether the message has been received and understood. Natural feedback is nearly always immediate. However, you can have an immediate feedback that is also deliberate. The key is to not purposely delay giving the feedback.

Delayed feedback involves an intentional pause. Perhaps the speaker is in the middle of a long explanation and it would be inconsiderate to interrupt him. Or perhaps there are multiple people involved in the conversation and someone else is giving their feedback first. Perhaps you think that if you wait for a bit, the meaning of the message will become clear. There are several reasons why someone might want to delay the sending of feedback. The important thing to note here, though, is that the act of delaying the feedback should be deliberate and intentional.

Now, when we talk about immediate and delayed feedback here, we are discussing it in the context of a face-to-face conversation. There is a whole different type of feedback (such as feedback on an assignment) where the immediate versus delayed conversation is much different. However, in the context in which we are operating — spoken conversation — immediate is what will most often be used.

No feedback is feedback

Let me ask you a question. If the receiver ignores the sender, is feedback being passed? Or perhaps the listener is not ignoring the sender, but there are barriers that thus far are insurmountable. Is feedback being passed here? Remember when we talked about ignoring way back in chapter 3? I mentioned that ignoring occurs when the message is received and decoded, but the receiver is making a conscious decision not to acknowledge it. In other words, Mr. R is deliberately making the choice to send no feedback. However, Mrs. S is still getting a message of some sort.

No feedback IS a type of feedback in itself. Suppose you pointed your television remote at your TV and pressed the "On" button and nothing happened. What does that tell you?

The fact that nothing happened indicates that the signal you sent from the remote never reached the television which was your target.   This concept works the same in communication.

The absence of a response tells the sender that the message, for some reason never achieved its intended mission.   It could mean that the receiver disagrees or is reluctant to accept the message.   It could mean that the receiver has hit one of the barriers to listening discussed in the previous section.

<u>*No feedback IS a type of feedback in itself.*</u>

How to give good feedback

As noted above, feedback is most effective when given deliberately.   This way you, as the listener, can give the right feedback that both matches the type of listening that you are engaging in and sends the correct response to your sender.   Here are some tips to help you give quality feedback.

- Remind yourself why you are listening
- Make sure you understand the message that the sender transmitted
- Make sure that your feedback is timely
- Make sure that your feedback is specific to the message
- Make sure that your feedback is informative
- Convey the return message (aka feedback) in a method which can be received and understood by the sender

Tips for Quality Feedback

Remind yourself why you are listening	Make sure you understand the message that the sender transmitted
Make sure your feedback is timely	Make sure that the feedback is specific to the message
Make sure that your feedback is informative	Convey the return message (aka feedback) in a method which can be received and understood by the sender

Remind yourself why you are listening.

If you've been following along through this book, you should be starting to understand that your "**Why**" of listening will direct what kind of listening you employ. Your listening type will factor into what feedback is needed. See how these things connect? By reminding yourself WHY you are listening you can clue into the kind of feedback that should be used in each situation.

Make sure you understand the message that the sender transmitted.

If you are not sure that you understood the message that the sender was communicating, your feedback should consist of clarifying questions. **Remember, the purpose of feedback is to let the sender know that the message has been received and understood appropriately.** If you did not understand the message, your feedback will and should be different than if you did understand.

> *The purpose of feedback is to let the sender know that the message has been received and understood appropriately.*

Make sure your feedback is timely.

Recall our discussion a earlier in this chapter about immediate versus delayed feedback? When employing active listening you should think about the timeliness of the feedback that you give. Should you stop the sender in the middle of speaking to give feedback or should you wait until they are finished? If you delay giving feedback the moment may pass and the sender may not know which message the feedback is in response to. On the other hand, immediate feedback could be construed as interrupting and could derail the speakers train of thought. Remember to consider the situation when timing your feedback.

Make sure that the feedback is specific to the message.

When you are considering the type of feedback to send, be sure to consider the message carefully and choose a response that matches it. If the message is positive, the feedback should be positive. If the message is negative, the feedback should match. You don't want to smile and nod if someone is telling you about their sick relative. This tip is more applicable to some types of listening than to others. For example, if you are employing appreciative or social listening, your feedback could be more vague. This is because you are not truly invested in the message that the speaker is sending. However, for most of the other listening types you should try to match your feedback to the message.

Make sure that your feedback is informative.

The purpose of feedback is to let the sender know if her way of delivering the message is working. If there is something that the sender could do to improve your understanding of the message, this is the time to share. Remember, Mr. R wants to help Mrs. S communicate with him more effectively. As a listener he has an equal responsibility in ensuring the success of the communication exchange. The more informative that the feedback is, the more improvements Mrs. S can make to her delivery of the message and the better the communication exchange can become. Thus, when you are formulating your response to your sender's message, be sure to think about the information that your sender might need and make your feedback as complete and informative as possible.

Convey the return message (aka feedback) in a method which can be received and understood by the sender.

Feedback is a return message. Whether it is verbal or nonverbal, when you give feedback to the sender, you are becoming a sender of your own message. Crazy thought, isn't it? The communication process is like a giant game of tennis, with the balls (messages) passing back and forth from person to person. When you return the Mrs. S's "serve" you want to do so in a way that gives her the best chance of receiving it. This may mean adjusting the tone of your voice or the words you choose to use. Think about all the barriers that exist for you as a listener. What barriers might exist that could get in the way of Mrs. S receiving and understanding your feedback? How could you help clear the channel for her?

When you give feedback to the sender, you are becoming a sender of your own message.

The Players

As each of our receivers navigates their WHY and employs the appropriate listening type, they must then send the right amount and type of feedback. This will tell the sender that the message was indeed heard and understood. Let's look at our six situations and see how each of the Smiths handles the feedback aspect of communication

Jarrod and Edna Smith (the romantic relationship)

Jarrod is watching the game. However, he sees that Edna is trying to communicate with him. Let's assume here that he has both received and understands her message. Now, he has two choices here. He could ignore her. Remember, no feedback is feedback in itself. What type of effect do you think that would have?

We talked earlier that feedback could be either positive or negative. What is an example of feedback that Jarrod might give that would be negative? What about positive? How might the type of feedback that Jarrod sends to his wife affect the future of the communication?

Jasmine Smith and her mother, Edna (the family relationship)

Jasmine is looking for feedback from her mother. She has come into the kitchen to tell Edna all about her upcoming date and ask for permission. What type of feedback do you think would be best for Edna to give — verbal or nonverbal? How do you think the feedback might be different if Edna just went with her natural feedback rather than used deliberate feedback? How might her natural inclination and feelings towards her daughter's message be different from the feedback she wants to give? Now think about the type of listening that Edna is using here. How would her feedback be different if she were using comprehensive verses emphatic listening?

Reggie Smith at college (the acquaintance relationship #1)

Reggie is once again an interesting case. As one of 150 receivers of the professor's message, how can Reggie provide feedback and complete the communication loop? Or should he? Would it be better for Reggie to give a delayed feedback? Would it make a difference if Reggie believed that he had understood the speaker's message in its entirety or if he is suffering from some semantic barriers?

The Smith's go out to dinner (the acquaintance relationship #2)

Jessica is invested in the message that Jarrod is sending — we've already established that. However, there are multiple barriers in place that could hinder her accurate reception of his message. How could using the appropriate feedback help her overcome some of those barriers? Could the right questions ensure that Jarrod knows whether his message about his order has gotten through and been understood? What are some deliberate types of feedback Jessica could use?

Edna Smith at the office (the work relationship)

Edna is giving complex instructions about a very technical project. It is important to her that her message be received and understood accurately. As a sender, what kind of feedback do you think Edna is looking for that will tell her whether her message is reaching her intended target? Do you think she is expecting the same feedback from Pam that she is from Tom? She has worked with Pam on many projects before, but this is her first time working with Tom. How could Tom use appropriate feedback to make Edna feel more comfortable working together? What kind of feedback should he give if he is having trouble understanding the parameters of the project?

Jarrod Smith and Mike, his golf buddy (the friendship relationship)

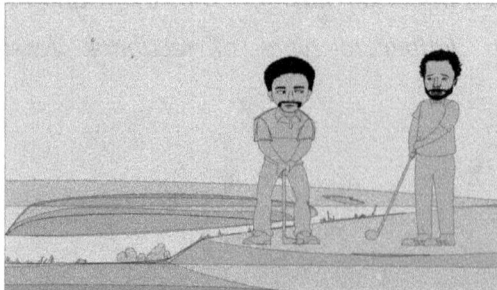

We established earlier that there are several types of listening that Jarrod could employ here. Let's focus in on two of them and see how feedback could be applied here and what the effect might be.

If Jarrod chose to employ appreciative listening, his feedback would likely consist of general verbal and nonverbal utterances. Perhaps an "I see" or a "You don't say". This would be just enough to assure his friend that he was listening without having to really be invested in the conversation. Do you think this type of response would be enough for Mike? Is that the kind of feedback he is looking for?

On the other hand, Jarrod may have chosen to engage in emphatic listening. In this case, his feedback will consist of more probing questions and focus more on his friend's emotional state. Jarrod might ask questions like "Why do you think she said that?" or "How did it make you feel when that happened?" What kind of difference do you think this type of feedback would have on Mike as opposed to the more general feedback?

Now, here is an interesting question. If Jarrod's goal is to end the conversation quickly (as it may be when you want to golf and your friend wants to bare his soul) what kind of feedback do you think would be best suited to that goal. How could Jarrod apply the deliberate application of feedback to both comfort his friend and speed up the conversation?

Chapter 9

Listening with your Eyes

"COMMUNICATION FORMS A SINGLE LANGUAGE THAT IS IN MANY WAYS RICHER AND MORE FUNDAMENTAL THAN OUR WORDS." - Leonard Mlodinow

Were you aware that in face-to-face communication, over 50% of meaning is the result of nonverbal cues? We so often talk about listening as something that is done with our ears. Perhaps this is because we so often look upon hearing and listening as synonyms. If you've been paying attention in this book, though, you now know that hearing and listening are two very different activities. Listening can involve not just paying attention to the input from your ears, but the input from all of your senses. It is just as important to employ active listening skills when listening with your eyes as when listening with your ears. Nonverbal means of communicating can often tell you more about the nature and meaning of the message than the actual words ever could.

Remember the factors of the communication process model? Nonverbal messaging greatly affects each one of these factors.

- **The Sender** must be aware that in addition to words, nonverbals are conveying a degree of honesty, competence, enthusiasm, and attitude about both the subject and about the receiver.
- **The Receiver** must acknowledge that without even knowing it's happening, messages are being sent *back to the sender* in the form of natural **feedback**, thereby altering the sender's delivery.
- **The nature of the message** itself is greatly influenced by the unintentional nonverbal messages being sent between the sender and receiver. It's the unintentional messaging can often have the greatest impact.
- **The channel or mode of delivery** includes both verbal and nonverbal. Even when there is no visual contact, such as a telephone conversation, nonverbals are being sent through Paralanguage (Voice)

Sometimes what you don't say speaks louder than your words. Nonverbals can either enhance or completely derail the entire communication situation. Regardless of the purpose or type of communication, learning to recognize and effectively manage what you are saying when you are not speaking ensures that people listen better to what you say when you are speaking.

Nonverbal Communication. What is that?

> *"The chimpanzees taught me a lot about nonverbal communication. The big difference is that they don't have a spoken language. Everything else is almost the same: kissing, embracing, swaggering, shaking the fist." - Jane Goodall*

Nonverbal communication is defined as a type of communication without the use of spoken language. It's the way we furrow our brow, pull on our ear, tap our feet, pace the floor, smile, frown, dress . . . any method we communicate with others in face-to-face situations. It includes the use of visual cues such as body language, distance and physical environments/appearance, voice and touch.

There are four important aspects of nonverbal communication we need to be conscious of whether we are sending or receiving messages. When these nonverbal signals match the words you are hearing or saying, they increase trust, clarity, and rapport. When they don't match, they can generate mistrust and confusion.

__When these nonverbal signals match the words you are hearing or saying, they increase trust, clarity, and rapport. When they don't match, they can generate mistrust and confusion.__

The four aspects of nonverbal communication include:

- Proxemics – or the use of space
- Paralanguage – or the use of voice
- Kinesics – or body signals
- Haptics—or the use of touch

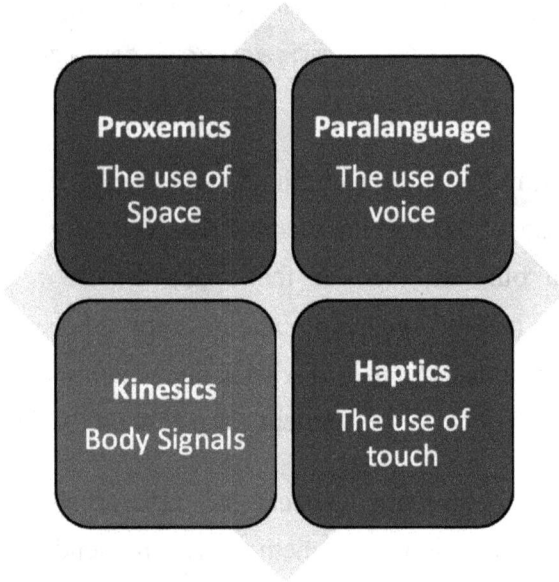

Proxemics
The use of
Space

Paralanguage
The use of
voice

Kinesics
Body Signals

Haptics
The use of
touch

Proxemics (Space)

Proxemics is a theory of non-verbal communication that refers to how people perceive and use space to further communication. Interestingly proxemic behavior is a learned behavior. We learn an understanding of the nature of space by observing those around us. Then, as senders, we use this behavior to illustrate, and sometimes take advantage of, a particular type of relationship.

Proxemics come in two types:

- Personal Space
- Physical Space

A sender can use both **personal** and **physical** space to communicate many different nonverbal messages. These can include positive signals such as intimacy and affection or negative signals such as aggression or dominance.

Personal Space

Personal Space is the distance we maintain when we interact with other people. There are several levels of personal space and each one is useful and appropriate in different communication situations.

- *Intimate distance* during private conversations only requires about 18 inches or less between the sender and receiver. This is reserved for very close family or friends. From there, the expected personal space increases as intimacy between people decreases.
- *Personal distance* is appropriate for casual conversation. This could be up to 4 feet.
- *Social distance* is between 4 and 12 feet and is more impersonal and is used in situations like an interview or small meetings.

- *Public distance*, which can be more than 12 feet, is appropriate in a presentation where the speaker is talking to many who are vaguely or not at all familiar.

Understanding the laws of personal space plays a huge role in communication. As a listener, when a speaker leans toward you, you feel more positive about that person. But if that same speaker steps in a little too close and your perception may view him as rude or inappropriate.

Distances of Personal Space

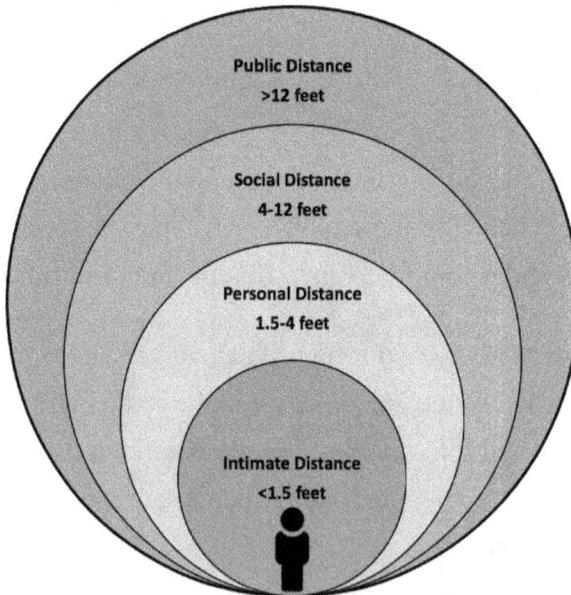

Public Distance
>12 feet

Social Distance
4-12 feet

Personal Distance
1.5-4 feet

Intimate Distance
<1.5 feet

Physical Space

Physical Space is the actual space that you perceive as belonging to you. An example of this could be your office cubicle. Often people use name tags, family pictures or trinkets to mark their office as their space. In certain situations, like office meetings or church services you sometimes find that each person will take the same chair from week to week. Even though these are open seating situations, it can become uncomfortable when a new member joins the group and is unfamiliar customary seating. This can apply in all sorts of situations where habit can imply ownership. How many of us have an accustomed place on our couch or at the dinner table? When a speaker inadvertently neglects the unspoken rules of our physical space it can cause barriers for the listener. He can become preoccupied with the space and it can be more difficult to focus on the message.

Paralanguage (Voice)

Types of Paralanguage

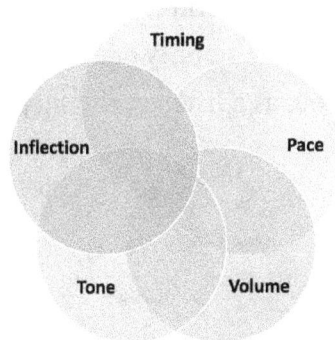

When we listen to other people, we often "read" the speaker's voice in addition to listening to the actual spoken words. Have you ever told your spouse or child, "don't speak to me in that tone of voice?" Or have you wondered if something said to you should be taken literally or as sarcasm? These are instances where you are using paralanguage to interpret the words actually spoken. Often this happens unintentionally, without the listener even being aware it is happening. However, too many miscommunications occur over paralanguage discrepancies. This is why, as a listener, it is important to take in the voice of the speaker, not just the words.

Paralanguage attributes you may pay attention to include the speaker's timing and pace, volume, tone, and inflection. These things together can give you, the listener, many clues to the true meaning of the message. Is Mrs. S telling the truth? Is she trying to hide something? Are her words calm, but her tone angry? Paralanguage can turn a compliment upside down or help a speaker deliver a hard truth.

Kinesics (Body Signals)

There are many body signals that amplify meaning between communicators. When considering nonverbal communication, the speaker's body can alternately amplify or contradict their message. Type of body language that you, as a listener, should pay attention to include:

- Gestures
- Eye Contact
- Facial Expressions
- Posture
- Locomotion

Types of Kinesics

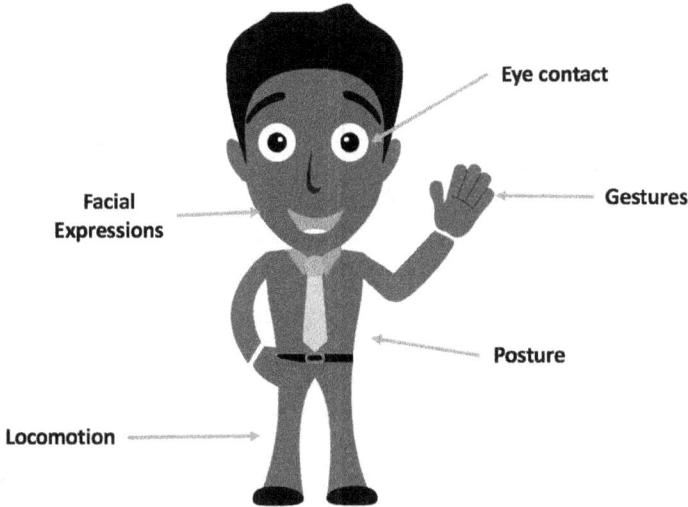

Eye contact

Gestures

Facial Expressions

Posture

Locomotion

Gestures

<u>Gestures</u> refer to the use of hands, arms, and fingers. Sitting with your arms folded can make you appear cold or distant. Random hand movements can make you appear nervous. How you angle your head, thrust your jaw, clench your fist, or lick your lips are signals that listeners use to interpret your meaning. As a listener, pay attention to the different gestures that the speaker is using. Also, be aware of what your gestures may be returning to the speaker as feedback.

It's also important to remember that gestures are not universal. Certain gestures are interpreted totally different in other cultures. Take the American gesture for okay – a circle with the thumb and forefinger. It is interpreted as an obscene or sexual gesture in Brazil and in some European cultures. In Japan, it says that something is overpriced. To the French, it means zero. In Tunisia, it's interpreted as "I'll kill you."

Eye Contact

Eye Contact refers to the way you look at someone when communicating. Like gestures, eye contact can infer many things, including interest, affection, hostility, or attraction. Reading your speaker's eyes will increase your perception of their credibility and confidence. People who are not telling the truth or who dislike the person they are addressing often drop their eyes. People who are bored tend to have eyes that wander as opposed to staying on the speaker. So, if you were speaking and your listener wasn't making appropriate eye contact, what assumptions would you make about his interest level? When you are listening, what are your eyes telling the speaker?

Like gestures, eye contact is judged differently in different cultures. In the American culture, when parents say, "look at me when I am talking to you," they are teaching their child a sign of respect. However, in many cultures (i.e., Native American, Latin American, and African cultures) it is disrespectful if the speaker is superior. There, averting the eyes is respect. In Japan, long eye contact is rude, disrespectful, and even threatening.

Facial Expressions

Facial expressions are one of the most important non-verbal cues in communication. Your expressions help communicate not only thoughts and ideas but also a wider range of emotions. Think how people communicate warning, fear, sexual attraction, and confusion without ever opening their mouth.

Interestingly enough, unlike other forms of body signals, many facial expressions are the same across cultures. The expressions for the big six emotions – happiness, sadness, anger, surprise, fear, and disgust – are the same no matter what culture you are in.

Common Types of Facial Expressions

UNSATISFIED   FRUSTRATED   ANGRY   SURPRISED (BAD)

SATISFIED   HAPPY   OVERJOYED   SURPRISED (GOOD)

PENSIVE   CONCENTRATION   PUZZLED   BAFFLED

DOUBTFUL   STRESSED   EXCITED   INDIFFERENT

Posture

Posture is an indicator of attentiveness, respect, and dominance. A loose posture can tell someone that you are relaxed. Too loose, though and you can appear uninterested or bored. On the other side of the spectrum a rigid posture can send a message of hostility.

Posture also includes body orientation. Face-to-face communication is direct body orientation and indicates more respect and attentiveness. Standing or sitting angles is indirect body orientation and can be interpreted as a different degree of respect or attention.

People often talk of posture in terms of open and closed. An open posture involves direct body orientation or orientation towards the speaker. Your arms are loose and relaxed. This tells the speaker that you are open and ready to listen. It communicates that you are prepared to receive the message that they are sending.

A closed posture, on the other hand, tells a quite different story. As Mr. R, having your arms crossed, your legs crossed, or facing angled away from the speaker may imply that you are not prepared to listen. It may signal your discomfort or disinterest to your Mrs. S.

Locomotion

Locomotion is the speaker's style of movement. Locomotion can be both motivated (intentional) or unmotivated (not intentional). Motivated movement helps clarify the speaker's meaning. The speaker could raise their arms to make her point. She could make her movements faster when she is talking about something intended to excite her audience. This type of movement focuses the listener on the speaker's message. Unmotivated movement, on the other hand, is distracting. Pacing is an example of unmotivated movement. The listener has a difficult time focusing on the message being passed and instead is focused on the locomotion of the speaker.

Haptics

Haptics refers to touch. Specifically, it deals with how and what touch communicates. This can be anything from a gentle touch on the forearm, a two-handed handshake, or a slight kiss on the cheek. Reaction to unsolicited touch varies from person to person. To some people a gentle touch on the arm may be comforting. To other people the same touch may seem threatening.

Acceptance of haptics also varies across cultures. Certain cultures in southern and central America and Southern Europe encourage frequent touching. Other cultures do not. There are Arabic countries where two people walking and holding hands is a simple sign of a friendship. However, in the US and several European and Asian it is interpreted as a much more intimate relationship.

How to Use Nonverbal Communication More Effectively

Nonverbal communication is inevitable. Whether in an intimate one-on-one conversation or in a lecture or presentation situation with hundreds of people, nonverbal communication is always occurring. The sender uses a combination of many methods of transmitting meaning. For you, the listener, body gestures, voice inflections, and use of personal space combine to sometimes tell you far more than speaker's words can. Remember, our emotions are almost completely transmitted nonverbally.

As a listener, it's important for you to realize that you are listening not only to the words being spoken, but to the nonverbals as well. Remember our discussion of the Barriers to Listening in Chapter 7? While listening to nonverbals is natural and necessary to the art of listening, misreading a speaker's nonverbals can **directly affect** the barriers that are getting in the way of effective listening.

In many instances, what comes out of someone's mouth and what she communicates through her body language are two totally different things. Just think back to the last time your spouse told you that they were mad, "not because of what you said, but how you said it." When faced with these mixed signals, the listener is left to choose between believing the sender's verbal or nonverbal message. In the same vein, the nonverbal signals you, as the listener are giving off can contradict everything that you are trying to send through deliberate feedback.

You can't control all of the signals you're constantly sending off. The harder you try, the more unnatural your signals are likely to come across. Below are some things you can do to minimize the conflict between your verbal and nonverbal messages when you are the sender of a message or of feedback. By recognizing the messages, you send with your body, you can also increase your ability to read those signals when you are in the position of the receiver. Here are some tips to help you be more effective in your use and interpretation of non-verbal communication:

Tips for Effective use of Non-verbal Communication

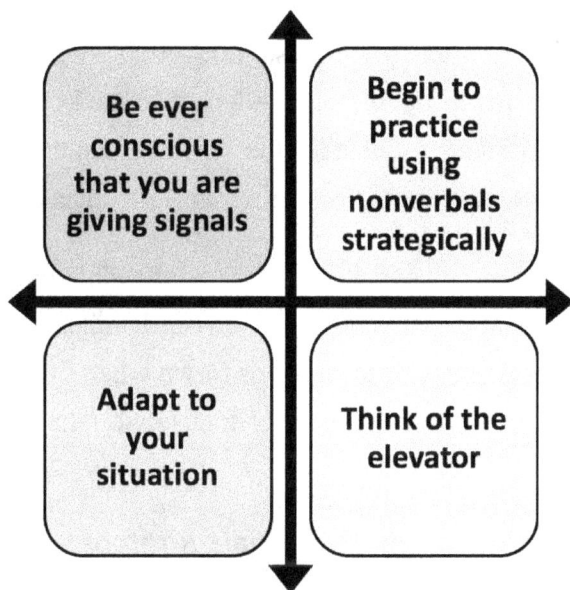

Be ever conscious that you are giving signals.

Think about this situation. You are in a meeting and are giving your side of a debate about the office budget. The meeting facilitator yawns and stares off into space. What does that tell you? Is she bored? Does she disrespect you or the message you are vocalizing? Is she distracted by personal situations going through her mind? Or maybe she is only tired from staying up to late last night. How does that make you feel as you explain your position?

Now,   imagine   what   these   actions   would   have
*on   your   speaker   when   **you**   are   the   listener?*

You can't begin to use non-verbal signals effectively until you acknowledge what your body is saying. Pay attention to your posture or your facial expression. Pay attention to how others are reacting to what you are not saying. Remember our discussion of feedback in chapter 8? These nonverbal signals that we are discussion now make up that immediate feedback we talked about there. It is important to consider the ways in which your nonverbal messages detract from your messaging, and practice changing habits.

For example, if you always clench your hands, put something (a note card, a piece of hard candy, a paperclip) in one hand. Practice smiling at regular intervals if you tend to scowl or frown when listening to people. If you tend to be an eye-roller practice focusing on the speaker instead.

Begin to practice using nonverbals strategically.

As you work on your interpersonal communication skills, decide on some nonverbal cues that will help accentuate the meaning behind your words. Practice using them intentionally until they fit your script naturally. Also pay attention to the nonverbal cues of others. Become a "people watcher". Intentionality of action will ensure that the feedback you intend to give is the message that your speaker receives. Practice your nonverbal cues just as diligently as you practice the spoken words of your conversations.

Adapt to your situation.

Be aware of your speaker. If your speaker is from a different culture than your own, some gestures and mannerisms could be misconstrued. Make sure, when you are interpreting the nonverbal cues of your speaker that you take cultural differences into consideration. Also, make sure that when you are giving feedback your nonverbal cues are appropriate not only to the message but to the receiver of your feedback. For example, many cultures interpret pointing as an insult. Some audiences could interpret a loud voice as excitement where others could see it as threatening. Of course, if all else fails, remember that eye contact usually trumps other non-verbals.

Eye contact usually trumps other non-verbals.

Think of the elevator.

In an elevator there is an unspoken agreement that you can safely invade my personal space as long as you do not make eye contact—everyone faces the door. On the other hand, when we are actively trying to communicate, many other nonverbal mistakes can be forgiven or forgotten if you **do** make eye contact with the other person. Eye contact tells someone that you understand that they are speaking directly to you and that your return message is for them specifically. Because of this, make sure that the person that you make eye contact with is the person that you want to receive your feedback. On the opposite side of the coin make sure that the person that you want to communicate with gets eye contact.

Whether you are the listener or the speaker in the communication model eye contact can make a world of difference in confirming to both sides that messages are being both passed and understood.

The Players

So, here we are again, with the Smith family. It's time to look again at our six situations. This time we are going to look at them in the context of nonverbal communication. How might each of our receivers "listen with their eyes" to help them better decode the message being sent?

Jarrod and Edna Smith (the romantic relationship)

Nonverbal signals could be huge in this conversation between Jarrod and Edna. Of course, this is only if Jarrod is looking. If he were watching Edna, he would see her hands on her hips and her eyebrows drawn together. Look at the picture, here. What can you tell about the conversation by looking at Edna's body language? What are Jarrod's nonverbal signals saying?

Jasmine Smith and her mother, Edna (the family relationship)

Examine, for a moment, the picture of Jasmine and her mother. If the entire conversation continued like this, what kinds of nonverbal messages are they sending to each other? Do you think this is an open, positive interaction, or could there be some barriers existing? What could Edna do so that she is sending uplifting nonverbal messages to her daughter?

Reggie Smith at college (the acquaintance relationship #1)

Reggie is far enough back, that his professor may not even see him to read any nonverbal feedback. However, Reggie's ability to read and interpret the professor's nonverbal cues may make a difference between true comprehension of the

instructor's message and confusion.   What types of nonverbal cues should Reggie be looking for?   What could the professor's posture and locomotion tell Reggie about his confidence level?

The Smith's go out to dinner (the acquaintance relationship #2)

Take a look at the picture of the Smith's at dinner. As a waitress, reading nonverbal cues could mean the difference between a large tip and no tip. In a crowded, noisy restaurant there may be more physical barriers to communication than in more private circumstances. Also, Jessica only has an acquaintance or stranger relationship with the Smith's. She does not enjoy the familiarity of nonverbal cues that a closer relationship may give her. How could Jessica use the idea of proxemics and facial expressions to help her achieve a more successful listening experience?   What could the nonverbal cues of Jarrod and his family tell her?   How could she have benefited from strategic practice of nonverbal communication?

Edna Smith with Pam and Tom at the office (the work relationship)

Take a moment to look at the picture for this scenario. Who do you think is the most comfortable and confident in this exchange? Is Edna giving off signals that she is an authority on her topic? Do Pam and Tom look like they are interested and really listening to what Edna is telling them? Knowing from earlier that Pam doesn't really think Edna is that competent to lead the team, what are some things she could do to make sure that her nonverbal signals do not give her true feelings away. How might she adapt to this situation so that Edna and Tom know that she is still taking this conversation, and this project, seriously?

Jarrod Smith and Mike, his golf buddy (the friendship relationship)

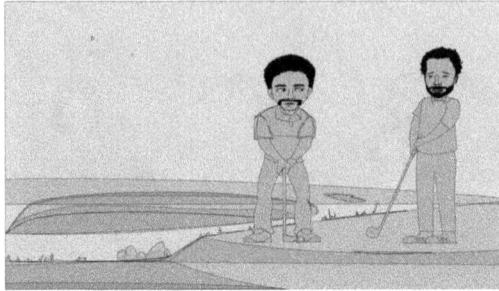

As we mentioned in the last chapter, Jarrod really just wants to play golf. However, he cares about his friend Mike and is genuinely interested in his friend's emotional well-being. Jarrod needs to be careful here. How could his nonverbal cues betray him in this situation? Look at Jarrod's expression in this picture. Think about it from Mike's point of view. What are Jarrod's facial cues telling him in this moment? What effect could that have on his relationship with his friend? What actions could Jarrod take to make sure that his nonverbal communication matches his verbal feedback?

Chapter 10

HOW to Improve your Listening Skills

"THE MOST SUCCESSFUL PEOPLE I'VE KNOWN
ARE THE ONES WHO DO MORE LISTENING
THAN TALKING." - Bernard Baruch

From the first time a person says "Mama," she begins learning to speak. Over the next few decades, she gathers knowledge and skill at public speaking, persuasive speaking, informative speaking, and any others that her profession or situations demand. Speech classes, counselor training, sales training are examples of the formal training available.

But did you know that only about 2% of us ever receive formal training for active listening? In the communication process, we are trained to be effective senders, but are left to figure out the receiving side by ourselves.

Throughout this book we have given you some great tips on how to think differently about the role listening plays in your life, your interactions, and your relationships. But now it's time to get to the business of really training ourselves to be better listeners. As you train yourself to be a good listener, it helps to have some clues to recognize what to practice. Let's focus on eight specific activities that you can practice to train yourself to be a better listener.

8 Activities to Improve Active Listening Skills

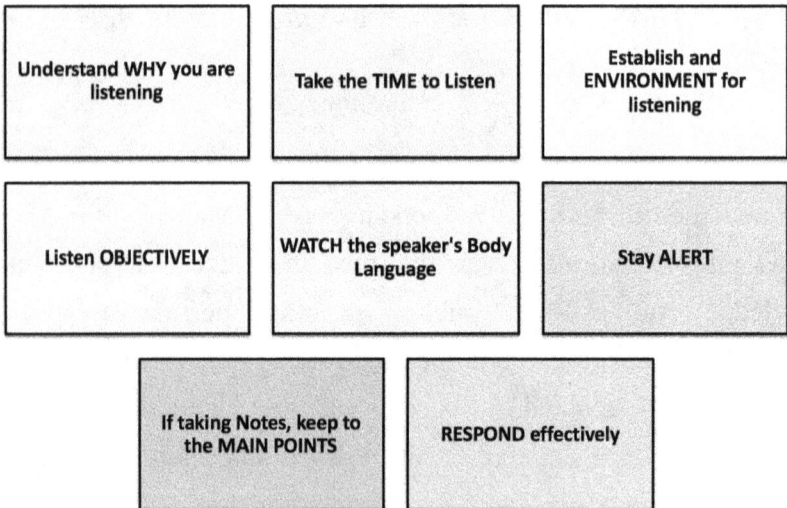

Understand WHY you are listening	Take the TIME to Listen	Establish and ENVIRONMENT for listening
Listen OBJECTIVELY	WATCH the speaker's Body Language	Stay ALERT
If taking Notes, keep to the MAIN POINTS	RESPOND effectively	

Activities to improve your active listening skills

Understand WHY you are listening.

Are you expecting to be educated or to be entertained? Perhaps you are listening to understand how to help someone else with a problem they are having? Understanding WHY you are listening enables you to adjust the type of listening required. The key, though, is to be honest with yourself about your why. Remember the 5 types of listening from chapter 6? To really be able to effectively choose the correct listening type, you must be able to be truthful with yourself about why you are listening,

<u>Understanding WHY you are listening enables you to adjust the type of listening required</u>

Take the time to listen.

Except for perhaps social listening, listening is time consuming. It requires sustained focus that often comes at the expense of something else. Active listening requires **motivation** to listen and effort to stay focused. Motivation is something that is seldom quick. Think about alternatives that you can do if you truly don't have the time available. Sometimes if you are unable to devote the time to listen, you can ask the sender to pick another time. Perhaps all you need them to do is pause for a moment so that you can move your attention from its current target and focus on the sender,

However, more frequently the situation dictates the need to listen at that moment. When that happens, you need to **stop what you are doing and take the time needed.**

> ### _Active listening requires_ motivation _to listen and effort to stay focused._

Establish an environment for listening.

The more you can minimize internal and external distractions, the better you will listen. Closing the door to reduce hallway noise, turning off the TV, or moving to a quieter location are simple, immediate steps you can take to ready your environment.

There are other physical and mental distractions that a good listener must also find a way to overcome. Your cell phone is perhaps the most common and noticeable physical distraction. If you are texting or checking Facebook, your sender must compete for your attention. Try to keep the phone down and your eyes on the speaker when they are sending you a message. You would hate to miss an important nonverbal cue because you weren't looking. The temperature in the room, an animated group of people a short distance away, a poor sound system are also physical distractions.

Mental distractions, such as the throbbing in that toe you stubbed, or wondering if you remembered to turn off the lights, are often more unpredictable and insidious distractors. Practice each day clearing your mind and focusing on the people you are speaking and listening to. Remember, the more you practice something, the easier it will get.

__Practice each day clearing your mind and focusing on the people you are speaking and listening to.__

Let go of preconceived ideas; listen objectively.

Do the speaker's ideas contradict what you were expecting or the way you believe? Do you know more about the topic than the speaker? Do your speaker's visual aids seem amateurish? If you are judging either the content or the speaker, if you are talking to yourself about your own point of view, you are impeding listening. These are some of the barriers that we talked about in chapter 7. Sometimes overcoming barriers, especially psychological barriers and biases, requires work and effort well before the communication begins. Let go of your preconceived ideas and allow yourself to truly listen to your Mrs. S, whoever he or she is. Open your mind as well as your ears to what is being communicated.

Watch speaker's body language.

Much can be conveyed through the speaker's mannerisms, enthusiasm, and voice inflections. Good listeners interpret what the speaker means. This means you need to practice listening to what is implied, in addition to what is said. If your co-worker says, "Don't worry about me, I'm fine," you may need more than their words to interpret the truth. Remember, sometimes we say the most without saying anything at all.

Stay alert.

Don't let your mind wander. Focus on what is being said rather than rehearsing how you will reply. A person can think at a rate of 400-800 words per minute. Most people speak at only 100 words per minute. Let that sink in for a moment. Your brain may be moving 4 to 8 times faster than the words coming from your speaker. That leaves a lot of free time for your brain. Make effective use of this difference in the time to think about and paraphrase what the speaker is saying.

Listening is an active endeavor. Frequently with a little forethought you can head off many of the issues that impede true communication. For example, if you find you have a tendency to interrupt, perhaps you are forming responses rather than listening. If you are imagining a Big Mac, you are letting your mind wander rather than listening. Both of these are times when you could use that extra time between the speed of their words and the speed of your brain to help get your mind back on track.

With a little forethought you can head off many of the issues that impede true communication.

If taking notes, keep to the main points.

If you're not used to it or good at it, taking notes can be distracting. When you are writing things down you are taking your eyes and your attention from the speaker and moving them to the paper (or tablet or computer or whatever you happen to be taking notes on). To help keep this to a minimum, listen for main points, key ideas, and facts. Only take notes on these items. If need be, you might try recording the presentation. That way you can take notes later and focus on the speaker in the moment.

If you are focused on getting everything down a paper, you are too busy writing to be evaluating and analyzing the message. Don't assume you need to remember every word. You need just the main points and some supporting facts. Remember, notes are usually just meant to jog your memory, not to replace your memory completely.

__Notes are usually just meant to jog your memory, not to replace your memory completely__

Respond effectively.

Use positive responses that encourage rather than interrupt speaker. Work on effectively using silent responses, such as nods or smiles, to tell your sender that you are listening. Ask probing or clarifying questions to tell the speaker that you are trying to understand and absorb the message. Like we talked about in chapter 8, the use of feedback can complete the loop and tell your speaker that either her message is getting through and being understood effectively or that she needs to adjust her delivery method. But quality feedback needs to be deliberate. You should practice each day being intentional in the type of feedback, both verbal and nonverbal, that you are sending.

__Practice each day being intentional in the type of feedback, both verbal and nonverbal, that you are sending.__

The Players

So here we leave the Smith family. We have walked with them as they navigated the many types of communications that go along with the relationships in their lives. Let's take one last look and sum up how each situation embodies the idea that hearing is not enough. Let's see how intentional strides towards being a better listener have helped the Smiths, their friends, coworkers and acquaintances have better interactions and relationships.

Jarrod and Edna Smith (the romantic relationship)

Jarrod and Edna Smith work on their marriage. They intentionally find opportunities to practice active listening, knowing that listening is a key component to nurturing a romantic relationship. While Jarrod is invested in the game he is watching, he knows that his WHY for listening to his wife is important. Therefore, he pauses his game and turns to face Edna. This allows him to clear the channel of the physical barriers to the message. Facing his wife lets him listen with his eyes as well as his ears. Because of this he notices the nonverbal signs of annoyance she is sending that contradict her calm and loving words.

So, what do you think? Did Jarrod take the trash out?

Jasmine Smith and her mother, Edna (the family relationship)

Edna also has been brushing up on her listening skills. She recognizes that she is tired from her long day at work. This may be causing some barriers to the communication between Jasmine and herself. However, she also understands how important it is that she utilize active listening in this conversation. Perhaps she asks Jasmine to wait until she finishes the cooking step that she is on so that she can make the time to listen to her. When she listens, Edna employs comprehensive listening so that she can later relate the information to her husband, Jarrod. She also intentionally tries to be objective and listen to her daughter with as little bias towards the topic as possible.

So, what do you think? Did Jasmine get to go on her date?

Reggie Smith at college (the acquaintance relationship #1)

Reggie has been working hard at improving his active listening skills. He knows that to do well in college, he needs to be an effective listener. He tries to choose a seat that will allow him to have a good view of the instructor. He wants to be able to see any nonverbal messages that the instructor may send along with the verbal ones. While Reggie knows he needs to take notes, he keeps the notetaking to the main points so that he can focus as much of his attention as possible on what the instructor is saying. He also makes sure to ask clarifying questions and give valuable feedback whenever possible, even though he intentionally delays his response until appropriate times in the lecture.

So, what do you think? Did Reggie pass the class?

The Smith's go out to dinner (the acquaintance relationship #2)

Both Jarrod Smith and Jessica the waitress understand the importance of listening. While Jarrod only appreciatively listened to the reading of the specials, he made sure to give appropriate positive feedback at the end. Jarrod understood that feedback also served to help maintain the connection and flow of the conversation. Jessica, on the other hand, was extremely invested and used comprehensive listening when Jarrod gave his order. She recognized and took steps to minimize the barriers that stood between her and accurate reception of Jarrod's message. She asked him to repeat the parts that she was not sure she understood.

So, what do you think? Did Jessica earn a good tip?

Edna Smith with Pam and Tom at the office (the work relationship)

Pam had a lot of barriers to work through. However, she had a solid Why and wanted the project to go well. It was difficult, though, for her to mask her nonverbal cues and Edna noticed that she was not listening as well as she could have been. Tom, on the other hand, employed effective critical listening skills. Even though he was new and had far less experience than Pam, he asked probing and clarifying questions. Pam, in comparison, mostly just nodded. Near the end of her presentation Edna had to decide who was going to be responsible

for which parts of the project.   In the end she gave Tom the more substantial share because she thought he had listened to the plans better and perceived him to have a more solid understanding of the project

So, what do you think?   Was the project a success?

Jarrod Smith and Mike, his golf buddy (the friendship relationship)

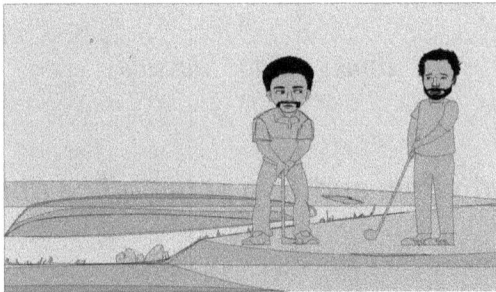

Good thing Jarrod has been practicing his emphatic listening. Even though they were supposed to be just golfing, his friend, Mike, really needed him today. Jarrod was able to recognize that he had some barriers to listening and intentionally worked to overcome them.   He made sure his nonverbal cues were soothing and gave feedback intended to comfort his friend.   Because of this, Mike soon felt much better.   Before long they were able to finish their golf game and their friendship relationship was stronger than ever.

So, what do you think?   Did Jarrod come in under par?

Chapter 11

A Few Last Words about Effective Listening

"Effective listening is the single most powerful thing you can do to build and maintain a climate of trust and collaboration. Strong listening skills are the foundation of all solid relationships." - Michelle Tillis Lederman

Remember our communication model from earlier? Let's take a look at it one last time.

Effective communications rely on both the sender and the receiver. Having a skilled and knowledgeable speaker is only half the equation. You could have a perfect speaker, an open channel, and a great message. However, without a **listener primed to receive the message**, there is no true communication. The skill and openness of the receiver are equally important in the communication process. This is where you come in. As the listener, you are **vital** to the process. Just like you are counting on the sender to be an effective speaker, the sender is counting on **you** to be an effective listener.

> *Without a listener primed to receive the message, there is no true communication.*

The Path to Better Listening

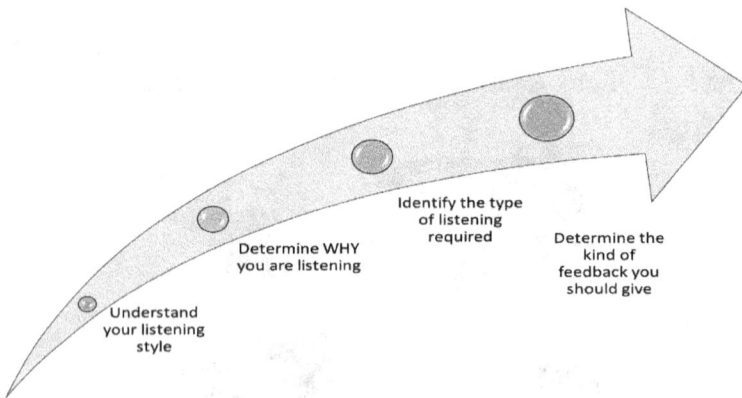

Understand your listening style

Determine WHY you are listening

Identify the type of listening required

Determine the kind of feedback you should give

To be an effective listener, you must:

To be an effective listener you need to follow the path. This path includes understanding what your listening style is and determining and deciding WHY you want to listen and why you are listening to the sender of the message. Then you need to take that information and use it to identify the type of listening that you should employ in that situation. Finally, knowing this you should intentionally determine what kind of feedback you should give and what message you want that feedback to give to the person with whom you are communicating. The path to effective listening may seem straight forward, but, as I hope you have discovered through this book, it can be anything but. Remember, to be able to walk the path confidently and accomplish the steps of effective listening you should be able to:

- Acknowledge that different situations demand different types of listening
- Use different sets of skills for the different situations,
- Understand the physical and personal barriers that could impede successful listening, and
- Realize that the sender is looking for your verbal and nonverbal feedback.

It is through these steps and through the practicing of some of the tips and tricks I have covered that you can begin to grow and develop your listening muscle. You will find yourself enjoying more positive communication experiences and more satisfying relationships as a whole.

The Players in Your Life

Throughout this book we used the Smith family as examples of the types of relationships that people encounter through their lives. Now it's time to think about the players in your own life.

Who do you share a romantic or a family relationship? How can you use your improved listening skills to grow even closer to those closest to you?

What about your Mike? In what ways can you be a better listener to your friends? When was the last time you really listened to them, past all the barriers and noise in our lives?

Consider your work relationships? How often do you let barriers and biases get in the way of real communication? How many opportunities have you missed because you weren't really listening? How many could you take advantage of now that you are?

Perhaps most importantly, how do you treat the acquaintances you encounter throughout your day? Are you only hearing them, or do you really listen to the people who cross your path? Which would **you** rather, that someone hears you or that they really listen?

Everybody that takes the time to speak to you has something they are trying to share. They have chosen a channel and are trying to pass a message. Every Pam, every Tom, every Mike, every professor, and every Jessica is trying to tell you something. They want to form a bond with you, if only for a moment, through their words. Whether or not you are listening – well that's up to you.

The Smith Family Relationships

Appendix

All the Best Stuff in One Place for Your Convenience

A s you made your way through this book, I hope you learned a lot about listening. It is my sincerest wish that you come out of this experience with a renewed appreciation of the role that listening plays in your relationships and your life.

I know though, that I presented a large amount of information in these pages. I included, intentionally, many lists to help you on your path to becoming a better listener. Now, because I like you so much, I am consolidating all my main lists and points into this appendix. I encourage you to give these a second look and a second and third thought. By applying the tips and tricks contained herein, you can become a better, more effective listener.

The Path to Effective Listening

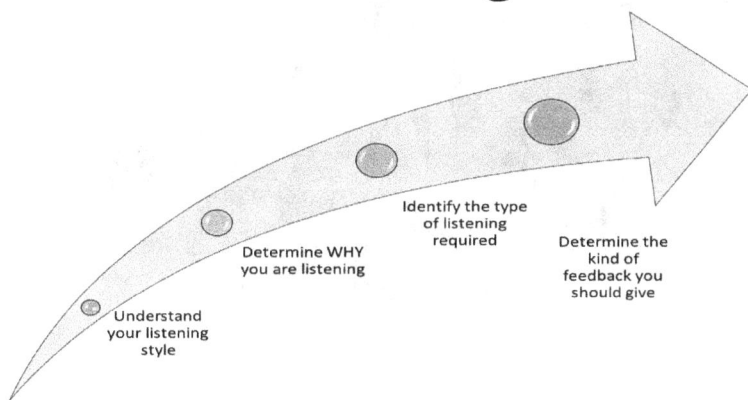

Understand your listening style

Determine WHY you are listening

Identify the type of listening required

Determine the kind of feedback you should give

The Relationship Continuum

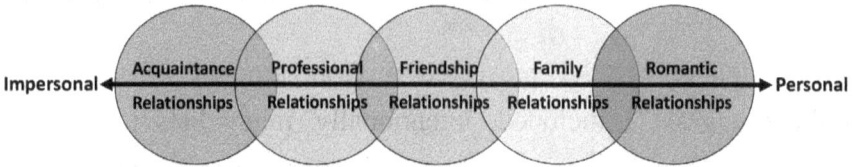

Impersonal ← Acquaintance Relationships | Professional Relationships | Friendship Relationships | Family Relationships | Romantic Relationships → Personal

The Communication Model

Hearing Vs Listening

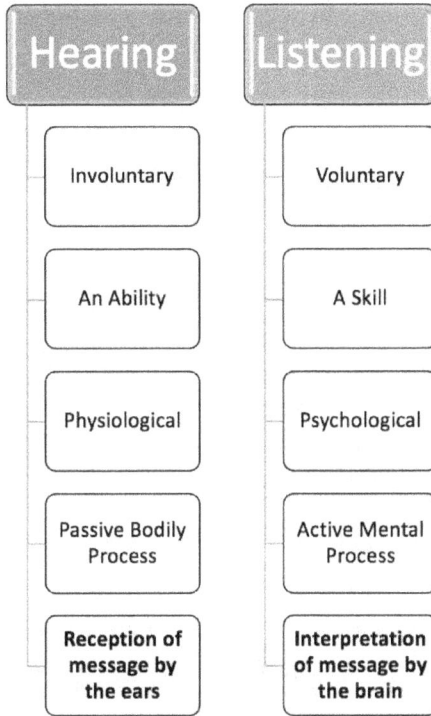

Hearing	Listening
Involuntary	Voluntary
An Ability	A Skill
Physiological	Psychological
Passive Bodily Process	Active Mental Process
Reception of message by the ears	**Interpretation of message by the brain**

Listening Styles

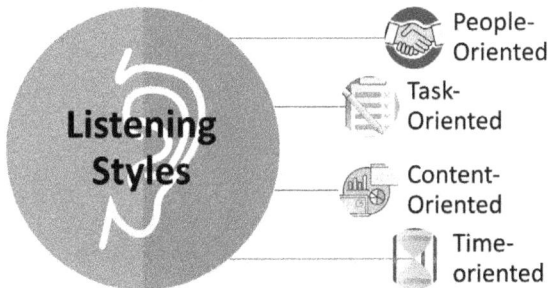

Listening Styles

- People-Oriented
- Task-Oriented
- Content-Oriented
- Time-oriented

10 Possible Motivations to Listen

1. We may want to listen because we are looking to obtain information that is important to us

2. We may want to listen because we are seeking to understand something

3. We may want to listen for enjoyment

4. We may want to listen to learn something

5. We may want to listen to be courteous or polite

6. We may want to listen in order to build or nurture a relationship with the sender

7. We may want to listen in order to solve a problem or prevent a problem

8. We may want to listen so that we can become more efficient and effective at something we are doing

9. We may want to listen to increase the sender's confidence in us

10. We may want to listen so that the sender will, in turn, listen to us.

Learning Styles Quiz

For each of the statements listed mark whether the statement is never true, seldom true, sometimes true, usually true, or always true.

		Never true 1 pt.	Seldom true 2 pt.	Sometimes true 3 pt.	Usually true 4 pt.	Always true 5 pt.
1	When listening to others, I focus on any errors in what's being said.					
2	When I am listening to someone I tend to smile, nod and affirm often					
3	I tend to withhold judgment about another's ideas until I have heard everything they have to say.					
4	When someone asks for my help, I wish they would give me just the facts instead of their opinions					
5	When listening to someone I tend to mentally fact check what they are telling me					
6	When people are talking to me, I tend to look at my watch or check the time					
7	When someone is asking for my help, I wish they would just tell me exactly what they want					
8	When listening to someone I often wonder where the conversation is headed					
9	When listening to others, I am mainly concerned with how they are feeling.					
10	The complement I most appreciate is you really seem to understand me					
11	I find it difficult to listen to people who take too long to get their ideas across					
12	When listening to others, I focus on understanding the feelings behind words.					
13	When listening to others, I notice contradictions in what they say.					
14	I prefer speakers who quickly get to the point					
15	I fully listen to what a person has to say before forming any opinions.					
16	When I am listening to a loved one, I wish they would remember that I have things to do.					
17	I enjoy listening to others because it allows me to connect with them.					
18	When listening to others, I consider all sides of the issue before responding.					
19	When listening to a presentation, I tend to catch errors in the speaker's logic					
20	I get frustrated when people get off topic during a conversation.					

People-oriented (add numbers 2, 9, 10, 12, 17)	
Task-oriented (add numbers 3, 7, 8, 15,18)	
Content-oriented (add numbers 1, 4, 5, 13, 19)	
Time-oriented (add numbers 6, 11, 14, 16, 20)	

8 Questions to Help Motivate you to Listen

Ask yourself each of the following questions. If you find yourself answering yes to more than a couple of the questions, it's time to **refocus your attention** and listen to what the speaker has to say.

1. Am I just pretending to listen . . . **when I should be listening?**

2. Am I seeking distractions . . . **when I should be listening?**

3. Am I criticizing the speaker . . . **when I should be listening?**

4. Have I stereotyped the topic as uninteresting . . . **when I should be listening?**

5. Have I prejudged the meaning and intent of the speaker's message . . . **when I should be listening?**

6. Am I avoiding the speaker's more difficult or complex topics . . . **when I should be listening?**

7. Am I formulating answers and follow-on questions during the speaker's presentation . . . **when I should be listening?**

8. Am I getting emotionally charged-up about some minor point the speaker made . . . **when I should be listening?**

5 Types of Listening

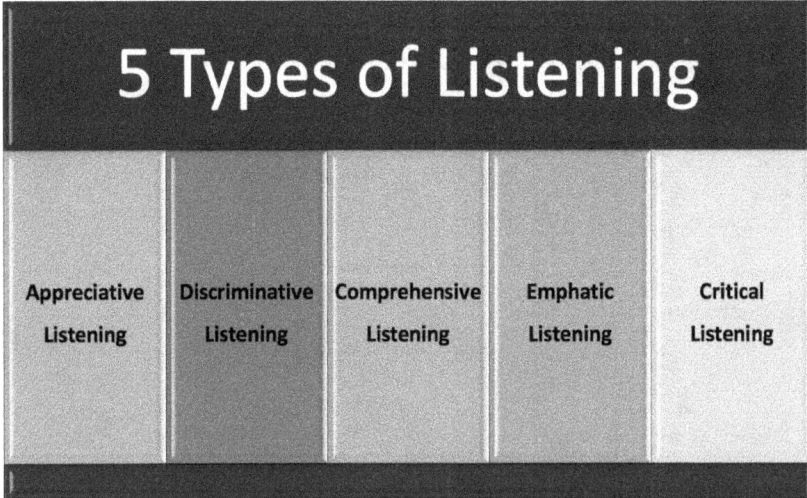

5 Types of Listening

| Appreciative Listening | Discriminative Listening | Comprehensive Listening | Emphatic Listening | Critical Listening |

Listening Type Flowchart

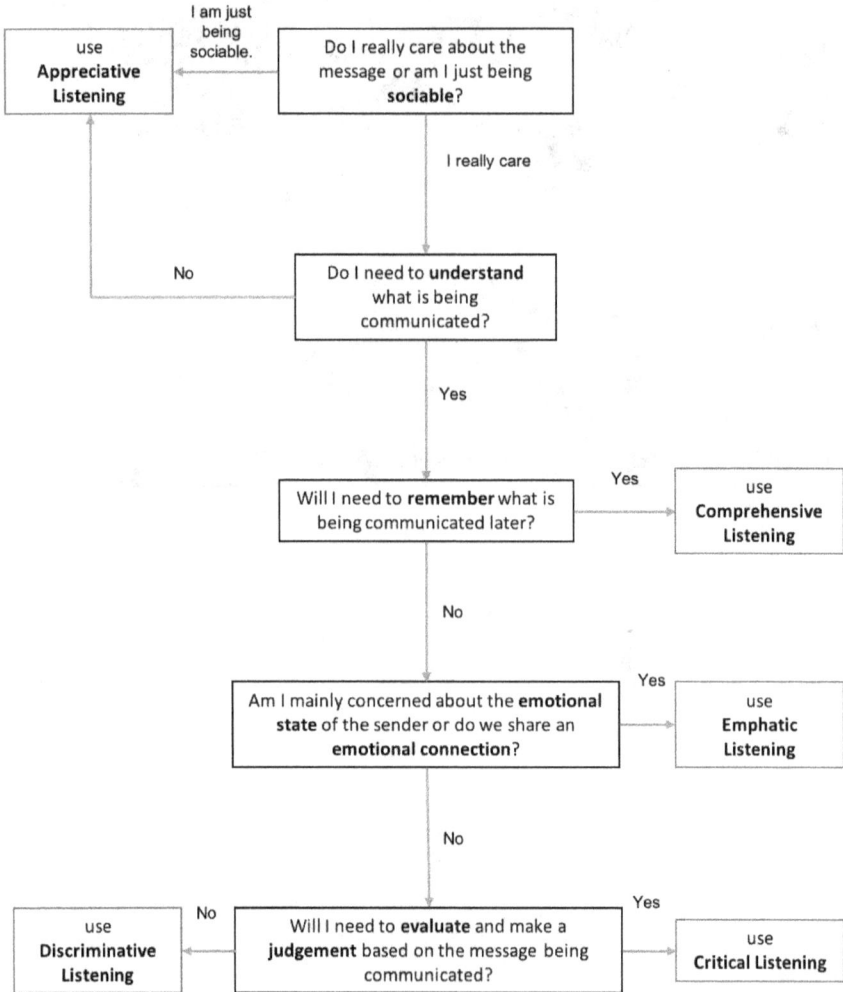

```
                    I am just
                    being
┌──────────────┐    sociable.    ┌─────────────────────┐
│    use       │◄────────────────│ Do I really care about the│
│ Appreciative │                 │ message or am I just being│
│  Listening   │                 │      sociable?      │
└──────────────┘                 └─────────────────────┘
        ▲                                   │
        │                          I really care
        │                                   ▼
        │                        ┌─────────────────────┐
        │         No             │ Do I need to understand│
        └────────────────────────│    what is being    │
                                 │   communicated?     │
                                 └─────────────────────┘
                                            │
                                           Yes
                                            ▼
                                 ┌─────────────────────┐   Yes  ┌──────────────┐
                                 │ Will I need to remember what is│──────►│    use       │
                                 │ being communicated later?│       │ Comprehensive│
                                 └─────────────────────┘       │  Listening   │
                                            │                  └──────────────┘
                                           No
                                            ▼
                                 ┌─────────────────────┐   Yes  ┌──────────────┐
                                 │ Am I mainly concerned about the emotional│──────►│    use       │
                                 │ state of the sender or do we share an│       │   Emphatic   │
                                 │  emotional connection?│       │  Listening   │
                                 └─────────────────────┘       └──────────────┘
                                            │
                                           No
                                            ▼
┌──────────────┐   No   ┌─────────────────────┐   Yes  ┌──────────────┐
│    use       │◄───────│ Will I need to evaluate and make a│──────►│    use       │
│Discriminative│        │ judgement based on the message being│       │Critical Listening│
│  Listening   │        │   communicated?     │       └──────────────┘
└──────────────┘        └─────────────────────┘
```

4 Types of Barriers to Listening (Noise)

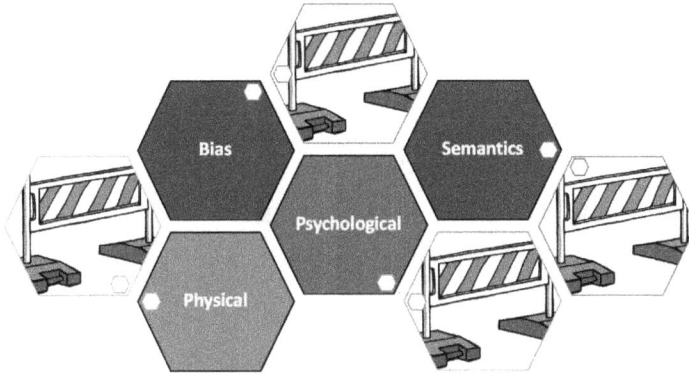

3 C's of Overcoming Barriers

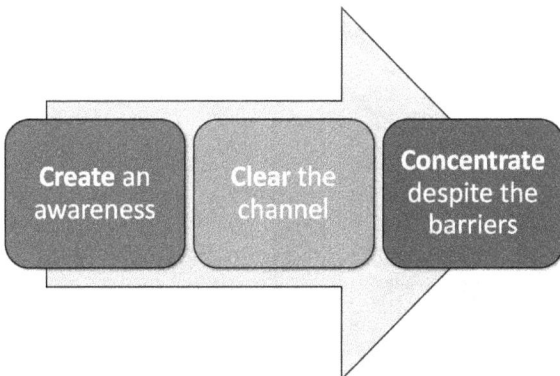

Questions to Help Create an Awareness of Barriers

1. Am I fully focused on the sender of the message or am I distracted?
2. Are there things in the environment that are distracting me?
3. Am I worried, stressed or anxious? Are my thoughts straying from the speaker and her message?
4. How do I feel about the speaker? Is it coloring how I am interpreting the message?
5. How do I feel about the topic? Is it coloring how I am interpreting the message?
6. Do I understand the words the speaker is using? Do I know what they mean?

Tactics for when you Find your Focus Slipping

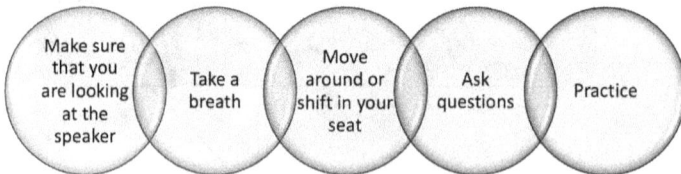

Make sure that you are looking at the speaker • Take a breath • Move around or shift in your seat • Ask questions • Practice

Tips for Quality Feedback

Remind yourself why you are listening

Make sure you understand the message that the sender transmitted

Make sure your feedback is timely

Make sure that the feedback is specific to the message

Make sure that your feedback is informative

Convey the return message (aka feedback) in a method which can be received and understood by the sender

Types of Non-verbal Communication

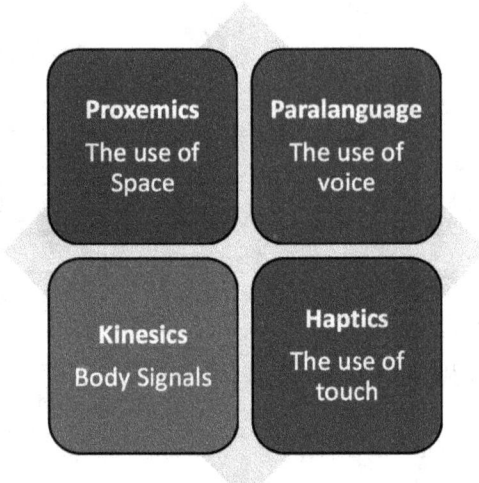

Proxemics
The use of Space

Paralanguage
The use of voice

Kinesics
Body Signals

Haptics
The use of touch

How to Use Non-verbal communication more effectively

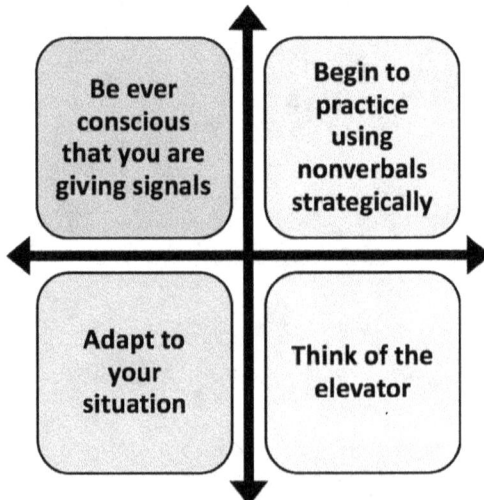

Be ever conscious that you are giving signals

Begin to practice using nonverbals strategically

Adapt to your situation

Think of the elevator

Types of Kinesics

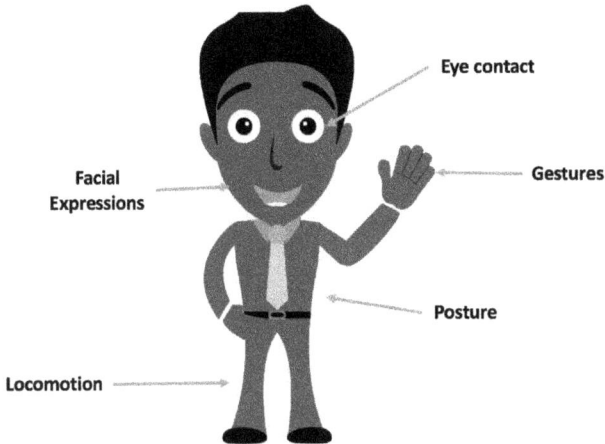

Eye contact

Gestures

Facial Expressions

Posture

Locomotion

8 Activities to Improve your Active Listening Skills

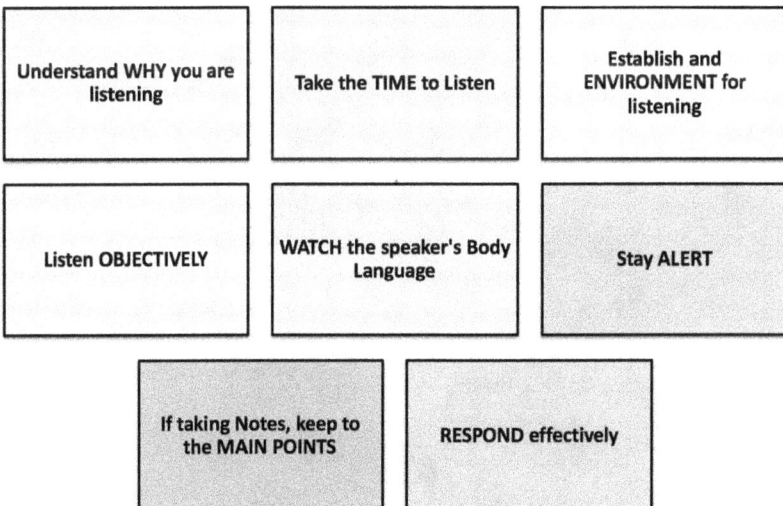

Understand WHY you are listening	Take the TIME to Listen	Establish and ENVIRONMENT for listening
Listen OBJECTIVELY	WATCH the speaker's Body Language	Stay ALERT
If taking Notes, keep to the MAIN POINTS	RESPOND effectively	

Glossary

Glossary

Acquaintance - a person who you know slightly but is not a close friend

Acronyms - an abbreviation formed from the initial letters of other words

Action-oriented listening - a style of listening behavior that is focused on the action or task that needs to be completed. See Task-oriented listener

Active listening - a pattern of listening that keeps you engaged with the speaker in a positive way

Appreciative listening - a style of listening behavior where the listener seeks certain information which they will appreciate. See social listening.

Barriers to communication - the things that get in the way of the passing of a message between the sender and receiver. See Noise

Biases - differences in personal feelings and beliefs about such things as age, race, gender, and personal appearance can alter the receiver's decoding of the message

Channel - the mode of delivery of communication messages

Closed posture - a posture oriented away from the speaker or with arms or legs crossed

Cognitive process - a process which includes thinking, knowing, remembering, judging, and problem-solving

Communication - the giving or exchanging of information

Communication Model - a visual representation of the communication process

Communication process - how the message goes from the sender to the receiver

Comprehensive listening - listening that attempts to not only understand but to learn from or remember the message

Content-oriented listeners - a style of listening that is more concerned with the facts themselves

Critical listening - a type of listening that requires you to hear, understand, evaluate and judge a message

Decoding - the process of interpreting the message in communication

Delayed feedback - feedback delivered after an intentional pause

Deliberate feedback - thought about and calculated prior to sending

Dialogue - conversation between two or more people

Discriminative listening - a type of listening that involves listening to the meaning of the message

Distraction - a thing that prevents someone from giving full attention to something else

Dominant listening style - the style of listening that a person employs a majority of the time

Emotional connection - strong feelings or intimacy for someone or something

Emphatic listening - a type of listening that involves not only understanding the message, but understanding how the sender feels about what she is saying

Environmental barriers - are items in the environment that are distracting

External distraction - distractions that originate outside the listener such as environmental noise

Eye Contact - the way you look at someone when communicating

Facial expressions - motions or positions of the muscles under the skin of the face

Family relationship - the people to whom you are connected to through some form of kinship, whether it is through blood, marriage, romantic relationships, or adoption

Feedback - the receiver's response to what the sender is saying

Friendship - a relationship with people whom we are not related to but choose to interact with on a regular basis

Gestures - the use of hands, arms, and fingers

Haptics - how and what touch communicates

Hearing - a physiological process that occurs when your ears pick up sound

Ignoring - an activity when message is received and decoded, but the receiver is making a conscious decision not to acknowledge

Immediate feedback - when the receiver communicates right away whether the message has been received and understood

Internal distraction - distractions that originate inside the listener

Interpersonal communication - the communication that we have with someone else

Intimate distance - a distance used for confidential communication of about 18 inches or less

Intrapersonal communication - the communication we have with ourselves

Jargon - words or expressions used by a particular profession or group and are difficult for others to understand

Kinesics - body movements and gestures

Listening - a cognitive process that involves decoding and attaching meaning to sounds

Listening proficiency - the level of skill with which someone employs listening

Listening style - manner in which an individual attends to the messages of another person

Locomotion - the speaker's style of movement

Mental distraction - distractions that originate inside the listener thoughts

Message - a short communication sent from one person to another

Motivation - the desire or willingness to do something

Natural feedback - is the immediate, spontaneous reaction to the message

Noise - the things that get in the way of the passing of a message between the sender and receiver. See Barriers to communication

Non-verbal communication - a type of communication without the use of spoken language

Open posture - direct body orientation or orientation towards the speaker

Paralanguage - attributes of speech other than the words themselves

People-oriented listener - a type pf listener who tends to be more interested in the person speaking

Personal distance - the distance appropriate for casual conversations

Personal Space - the distance we maintain when we interact with other people

Physical Barriers - types of noise that are direct environmental interferences

Physical distraction - the bodily things that get in the way of communication

Physical Space - the actual space that you perceive as belonging to you

Physiological barriers - the physical things going on with our body that may be distracting

Physiological process - a process in which the organ systems work together to acomplish a goal

Posture - the position in which we hold our bodies

Pragmatic problems - issues that relate to matters of fact and practical affairs

Professional or work relationship - a relationship formed with people with whom you have a professional connection

Proxemics - a theory of non-verbal communication that refers to how people perceive and use space to further communication

Psychological Barriers - the things going on in the listener's mind that interfere with the interpretation of the message

Public distance - the appropriate distance of a presentation or lecture

Receiver - the intended recipient of the message

Reciprocal - given, felt or done in return

Relational Bond - the social, emotional or cognitive connection between two people

Relationship - the manner in which two people are connected

Relationship Continuum - the range in which relationships can fall going from impersonal to personal

Romantic relationship - in which you feel very strongly attracted to the other person, both to their personality and, often, physically

Semantic Barriers - when the sender uses words that the receiver doesn't understand

Semantics - the study of the meanings of words and phrases

Sender - the speaker or person transmitting the message

Social distance - the distance appropriate for interviews or small meetings. About 4-12 feet

Social listening - a style of listening behavior where the listener seeks certain information which they will appreciate. See appreciative listening.

Task-oriented listeners - a type of listener that is focused on the action or task that needs to be completed. See Action-oriented listener

Time-oriented listeners - a style of listening behavior where the listener prefers messages that are short and to the point due to time constraints or limited attention spans

Verbal message - communication which uses words or sounds

Index

Index

Symbols

3 C's of Overcoming Barriers 92, 167

A

Acquaintances 11, 12

Acronyms 89, 90, 99

Active listening 3, 4, 38, 41, 42, 60, 93, 108, 117, 139, 140, 146, 147, 148

Appreciative listening 69, 70, 71, 73, 175

Aristotle 45, 46

Awareness of the Barriers 92

B

Barriers 16, 17, 41, 46, 58, 76, 80, 85, 86, 87, 88, 89, 90, 91, 92, 93, 94, 95, 96, 97, 98, 99, 100, 103, 105, 106, 110, 113, 123, 130, 135, 136, 143, 146, 147, 149, 150, 153, 154, 177, 180

Baruch 139

Biases 87, 90, 175

C

Channel 16, 38, 72, 92, 93, 98, 110, 118, 146, 152, 154

Cognitive process 36, 40, 178

Communication Model 15, 160, 176

Comprehensive listening 69, 72, 176

Content-oriented listeners 46, 50, 176

Conversation 9, 27, 30, 53, 54, 55, 65, 88, 95, 97, 99, 100, 105, 114, 115, 118, 121, 129, 134, 135, 137, 147, 149, 176

Covey 67

Critical listening 69, 75, 76, 176

D

Dansky 25

Delayed feedback 104, 176

Deliberate feedback 104, 176

Discriminative listening 69, 71, 73, 176

Distraction 142, 177, 178, 179, 180

Dominant 51, 177

Dominant listening style 47, 49, 51

E

Edna Smith 19, 21, 23, 29, 32, 40, 42, 52, 55, 62, 65, 79, 80, 82, 96, 99, 111, 113, 134, 137, 146, 149

Emphatic listening 69, 73, 74, 75, 177

Environmental barriers 88, 177

Epicitus 4

Eye Contact 124, 126, 177

F

Face-to-face communication 117

Facial Expressions 124, 126, 127

Family relationships 11, 13

Feather 45

Feedback 4, 16, 17, 29, 31, 33, 39, 40, 52, 70, 74, 75, 95, 101, 102, 103, 104, 105, 106, 108, 109, 110, 111, 112, 113, 114, 115, 118, 125, 130, 132, 133, 135, 138, 145, 148, 149, 150, 153, 176, 178, 179

Freedom to speak 2

Friendships 11, 12

G

Gates 101

Gestures 124, 125, 178

Goodall 119

H

Haptics 120, 129, 178

I

Ignoring 38, 178

Immediate feedback 104, 178

intentional action 92

Interpersonal communication 8, 9, 178

Intimate distance 121, 178

Intrapersonal communication 8, 9, 178

J

Jackson 35

Jargon 89, 90

Jarrod Smith 19, 21, 23, 29, 32, 40, 42, 52, 55, 62, 65, 79, 80, 82, 96, 99, 111, 113, 134, 137, 146, 149

Jasmine Smith 20, 30, 40, 53, 63, 80, 96, 112, 135, 147

K

Kinesics 120, 124, 125, 178

L

Lederman 151

Lippmann 1

Listening Style 45, 47

Locomotion 124, 128, 179

M

Message 2, 7, 8, 9, 10, 16, 17, 20, 29, 30, 31, 36, 38, 39, 40, 41, 42, 43, 49, 50, 52, 54, 55, 56, 57, 59, 61, 65, 67, 68, 70, 71, 72, 73, 74, 75, 76, 77, 79, 80, 82, 86, 87, 88, 89, 90, 91, 92, 93, 94, 95, 96, 100, 102, 103, 104, 105, 106, 108, 109, 110, 111, 112, 113, 114, 117, 118, 123, 124, 128, 129, 130, 131, 132, 133, 134, 136, 142, 144, 145, 146, 149, 152, 153, 154, 164, 168, 175, 176, 177, 178, 179, 180, 181, 190

Mlodinow 117

Motivate 61, 164

Motivation 49, 50, 60, 62, 64, 65, 141

Mr. R 16, 57, 67, 68, 73, 76, 86, 87, 90, 91, 101, 102, 105, 109, 128

Mrs. S 16, 57, 67, 68, 70, 71, 72, 73, 74, 75, 76, 86, 87, 90, 91, 95, 101, 102, 104, 105, 109, 110, 124, 128, 143

N

Natural feedback 104, 179

Negative feedback 103

Networking 25

No feedback 105, 106

Noise 16, 36, 85, 86, 87, 94, 97, 142, 154, 177, 180

Non-verbal 103, 131, 169, 170, 179

Nonverbal cues 71, 74, 93, 104, 117, 132, 133, 135, 136, 137, 149, 150

Non-verbal feedback 103

O

Orben 85

P

Paralanguage 118, 120, 123, 124, 179

Partnership 13, 17

Passive process 38

People-oriented listeners 46, 49

Personal distance 121, 179

Personal Space 121, 122, 179

Physical barriers 87, 88

Physical Barriers 87, 180

Physical Space 121, 122, 180

Physiological barriers 88

Physiological process 35, 36, 178

Players 18, 29, 40, 52, 62, 79, 95, 111, 134, 145, 154

Positive feedback 103

Posture 124, 128, 180

Pragmatic problems 92, 93

Preconceived ideas 143

Professional Relationships 12

Proxemics 120, 121, 180

Psychological Barriers 87, 89, 180

Public distance 122, 180

R

Receiver 9, 10, 16, 17, 36, 38, 39, 42, 57, 58, 67, 68, 74, 76, 79, 86, 87, 89, 90, 91, 102, 103, 104, 105, 106, 118, 121, 130, 133, 152, 175, 176, 177, 178, 179, 181

Reggie Smith 21, 31, 41, 54, 64, 80, 97, 112, 135, 148

Relational Bond 11, 181

Relationship 2, 3, 10, 11, 12, 13, 14, 15, 17, 19, 20, 21, 22, 23, 24, 29, 30, 31, 32, 33, 40, 41, 42, 43, 52, 53, 54, 55, 56, 60, 62, 63, 64, 65, 66, 74, 79, 80, 81, 82, 96, 97, 98, 99, 100, 104, 111, 112, 113, 114, 121, 129, 134, 135, 136, 137, 138, 146, 147, 148, 149, 150, 154, 162, 177, 180, 181

Relationship Continuum 14, 160, 181

Relationships 1, 2, 3, 4, 10, 11, 12, 13, 14, 15, 19, 27, 49, 53, 54, 71, 72, 104, 139, 146, 151, 153, 154, 159, 177, 181

Remen 57

Rhetoric 45

Romantic Relationships 13

S

Semantic Barriers 87, 89, 181

Sender 9, 16, 17, 39, 42, 49, 57, 59, 60, 65, 67, 68, 72, 73, 74, 75, 76, 77, 82, 86, 89, 91, 92, 94, 95, 102, 103, 104, 105, 106, 108, 109, 110, 111, 114, 118, 121, 129, 130, 141, 142, 145, 152, 153, 162, 168, 175, 176, 177, 179, 181

Social distance 121, 181

Social listening 70, 74, 109, 141, 175

Speech 17, 139

Stephens Minister 68

Stereotyped 61, 64, 164

Symbolic behavior 7

T

Task-oriented listeners 46, 181

Time-oriented listeners 46, 181

Turner 7

Types of Listening 67, 165

V

Verbal feedback 102

Visual interferences 88

W

Work relationships 12, 154

About Exploring Expression

About Brandy Champeau

Brandy Champeau is a speaker, author and curriculum developer from Coastal Georgia. She is also the founder and CEO of Exploring Expression LLC. Brandy has written several books for both children and adults and has developed curriculum for all ages and types from toddlers and preschool children to college students to adults and government agencies. She is a trained communicator with decades of experience in both speaking and, more importantly, listening.

About Nancy Holt

Nancy Holt is the co-owner and business manager of Exploring Expression LLC. Prior to this role she spent several decades in various positions of leadership and management. Nancy learned early on that the number one skill for any leader is communication, both in oral and written forms. She often had the opportunity to teach leadership and communication skills to younger audiences. Her common theme was that regardless of how competent of a writer or speaker you are, if you can't listen, you can't lead.

About Exploring Expression

Exploring Expression LLC was founded to help parents, caregivers or educators of K12 students become the very best expression of themselves so that they can make learning fun, easy and natural not just for their children, but for themselves as well.

Exploring Expression focuses on 3 specific offerings:

1. We build quality learning resources for K12 students

2. We create resources for parents and educators to help them become the best expressions of themselves and equip them to better facilitate learning opportunities for their children

3. We utilize public speaking platforms to spread the message of becoming the best expression of yourself through the cultivation of a learning lifestyle

As you can see, our focus is learning. Learning about yourself and learning about the world. Self-improvement and education. Because in the end it all comes down to learning. It's time to rethink how we think about learning. Learning doesn't have to be hard and it doesn't have to be boring. At Exploring Expression, we want to help you put the engagement and excitement back into education and to put the education back into life.

Available Now at ExploringExpression.com or on Amazon

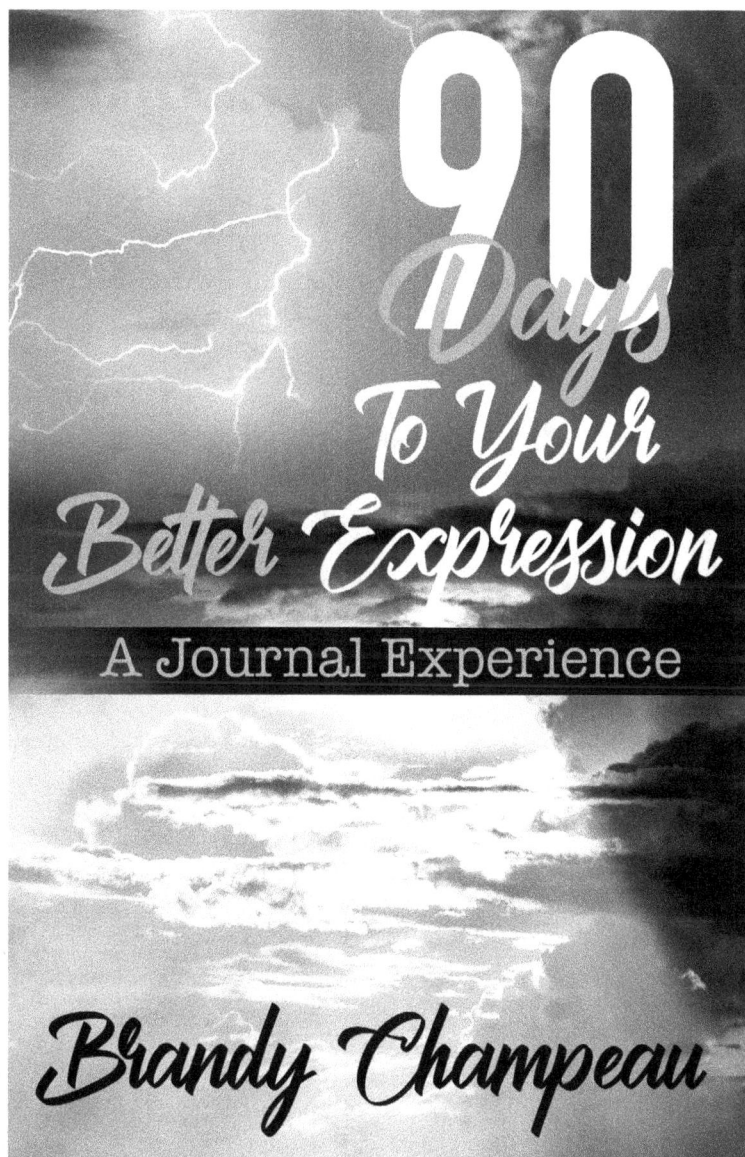

Available Now at ExploringExpression.com or on Amazon

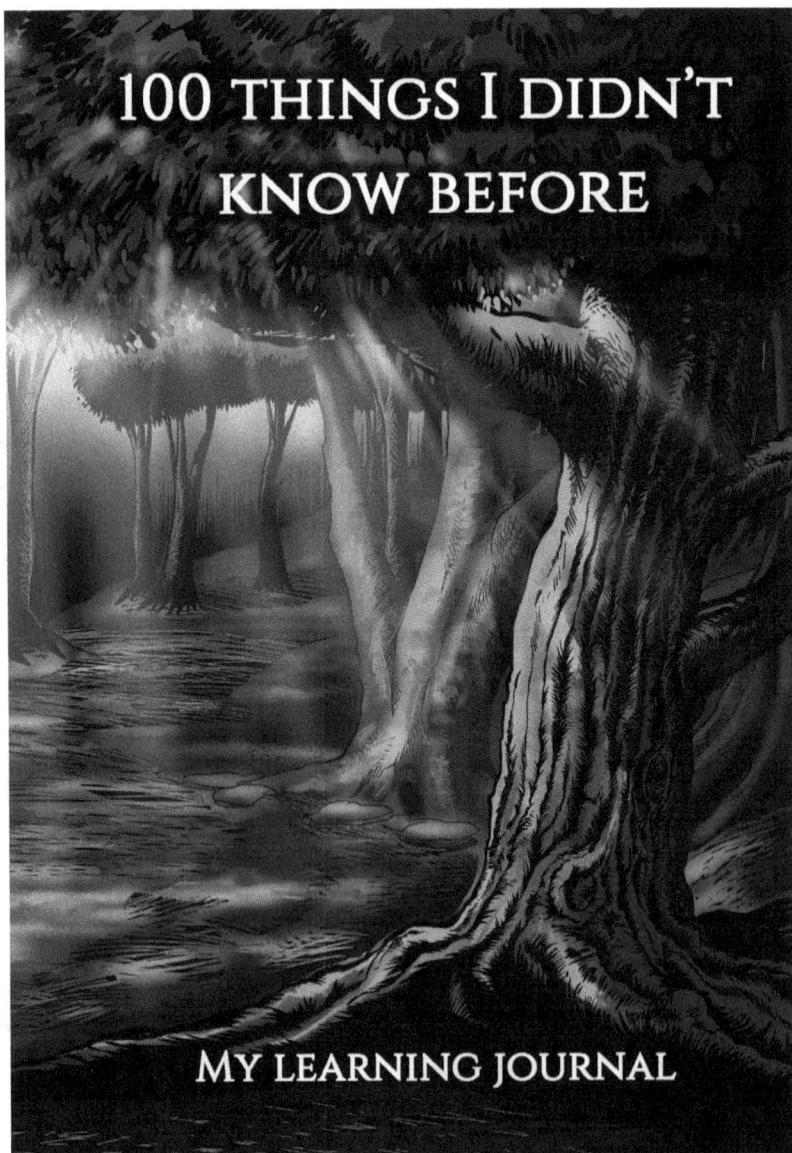

Check out these Children's Books and Workbooks by Brandy Champeau.

Available at ExploringExpression.com or on Amazon

Exploring Expression

Connect with Us

We would love to hear from you!

htpps://ExploringExpression.com

ExploringExpression@gmail.com

https://www.facebook.com/ExploringExpression

https://www.instagram.com/ExploringExpression

https://www.twitter.com/ExExAdmin

https://www.pinterest.com/ExploringExpression

https://youtube.com/channel/UC7xXoQ60I2fsGLuMH16q1_w

www.ingramcontent.com/pod-product-compliance
Lightning Source LLC
Chambersburg PA
CBHW070913270326
41927CB00011B/2548